50 Simple Ways to Pamper Your Cat

Arden Moore

BARNES
&NOBLE
BOOKS
NEW YORK

Contents

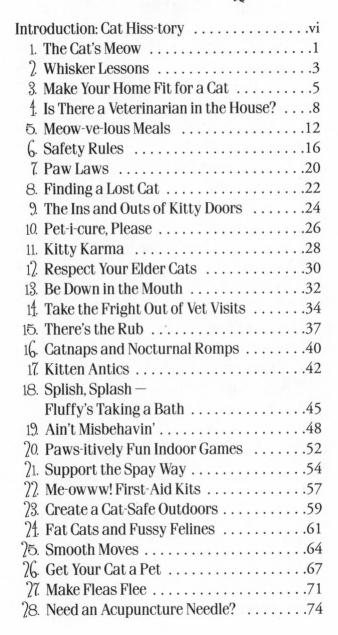

Introduction: Cat Hiss-tory vi

1. The Cat's Meow .1
2. Whisker Lessons 3
3. Make Your Home Fit for a Cat 5
4. Is There a Veterinarian in the House? 8
5. Meow-ve-lous Meals 12
6. Safety Rules .16
7. Paw Laws 20
8. Finding a Lost Cat 22
9. The Ins and Outs of Kitty Doors 24
10. Pet-i-cure, Please 26
11. Kitty Karma .28
12. Respect Your Elder Cats 30
13. Be Down in the Mouth 32
14. Take the Fright Out of Vet Visits 34
15. There's the Rub 37
16. Catnaps and Nocturnal Romps 40
17. Kitten Antics .42
18. Splish, Splash —
    Fluffy's Taking a Bath 45
19. Ain't Misbehavin' 48
20. Paws-itively Fun Indoor Games 52
21. Support the Spay Way 54
22. Me-owww! First-Aid Kits 57
23. Create a Cat-Safe Outdoors 59
24. Fat Cats and Fussy Felines 61
25. Smooth Moves 64
26. Get Your Cat a Pet 67
27. Make Fleas Flee 71
28. Need an Acupuncture Needle? 74

29. Purr-fect Herbs 76
30. Cruising with Your Kitty 79
31. Making the Skies Friendlier 83
32. The Inside Scoop on Litter 87
33. Cat Scratch Fever 90
34. Paw-ticulars on Hotel Lodging 92
35. Seafaring Cats 94
36. Get into the Spirit 96
37. Good Toys, Bad Toys 98
38. Climatize Your Cat 101
39. Catnip Clues 103
40. Lend a Paw 105
41. Kitty Cuisine 107
42. Brush Up on Your Grooming Skills 111
43. Pet Insurance 114
44. Picking a Pet-Pleasing Sitter 116
45. Home Alone 119
46. Meowy Christmas and
    Other Holidays 122
47. 10 Cat Commandments 125
48. Super Supplements 127
49. 'Net Surfin' with Your Cat 131
50. Catty Remarks .133
Index 135

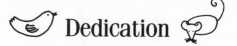# Dedication

To all the funny, fussy, and friendly felines
who have enriched my life and taught
me never to stereotype a cat.
Each is unique.
Special mention goes to Callie,
Little Guy (a.k.a. Dude),
and Murphy.

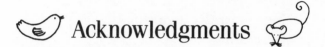# Acknowledgments

I wish to thank all the veterinarians, animal behaviorists, animal shelter directors, and cat owners who generously shared their ideas for making this world a better place for our feline friends. Special thanks to my editor, Deborah Balmuth, for giving me this delightful opportunity to offer pampering tips to cat fans everywhere.

Cat Hiss-tory

About five thousand years ago, long before the invention of the litter box, cats finally agreed to be domesticated. They waited 15 thousand years or so after the dog was tamed just to make sure it was worth mingling with people.

Cats cleverly learned from the mistakes of dogs. No way would they automatically heed such commands as "come," "sit," or "heel." Pull a sled through snow? I don't think so. Tolerate weekly baths? Nice try.

Cats live their nine lives by three simple rules:

1. Never grovel.
2. Never sacrifice dignity.
3. Never lie.

From the beginning, cats established a partnership with people. Ancient Egyptian pharaohs elevated their feline companions to nearly godlike status. The once-uncharted seas were made tolerable for sailors when cats went onboard. Cats have prowled the White House since the days of Abraham Lincoln.

Magically, cats won us over, and their popularity continues to soar. At last count, about 64 million cats were members of American households.

So, it's time we're honest with ourselves. Deep down inside, we know our cats deserve a book on pampering. In fact, if you ask them, they'll candidly tell you that this book is long overdue. Make each and every day of your feline's life (or lives!) the cat's meow.

Paws Up!

Arden Moore

The Cat's Meow

Cats are capable of making as many as 20 meow sounds. Each conveys a distinctive message that can easily be misinterpreted by humans. Unfortunately, it is unlikely that anyone will ever publish a *Berlitz Guide to Cat Chat*. But you can flatter your feline by learning Catspeak.

Say What?

Here are some translation tips to prevent you from committing any feline faux pas.

Mew. Tiny sounds spoken by young kittens, usually seeking food or warmth.

Chirp. This musical trilling sound seems to end in a question mark and usually means a friendly greeting, such as "welcome home."

Meow. Your cat is commanding your immediate attention. She may be declaring, "You're late with breakfast" or "Come see me play — *now.*"

Hiss. Plain and simple, this sinister sound means "back off."

Purr. Some cats craft noises that sound like distant thunderstorms. Others deliver purrs that resemble full-throttle Mack trucks. No one is positively sure how a cat purrs, but cats have a knack for breathing in and out while purring with their mouths closed. Strangely, cats purr when contented and, occasionally, when faced with a stressful situation, such as a vet visit.

Cats are good at understanding us. Your cat understands voice tone much better than any specific word. Although my cats seem to know the word *treat* even when I spell it out!

Chat with your cat often in soothing, flattering tones so she won't feel neglected.

Use your cat's name every time you talk to her so that she recognizes it. Most cats will soon realize that their names are associated with good things, such as praise, petting, or treats.

Whisker Lessons

Interpreting cat vocals gets you only partway across the bridge of communication. To truly cater to your cat's needs, you need to understand her body language: how she moves, how she smells, what she sees, how she hears, and why she needs whiskers.

The Rubdown

Why does your cat rub her cheeks against your leg? She is marking you — it's her way of declaring to others, "Hey, this is *mine*." Don't worry; this isn't the same type of mark that some cats make when they spray urine. Only other animals can pick up the scent.

When two cats give each other full-body rubs, the action translates into: "There's strength in numbers; let's create a group odor for identification."

Learn Other Cat Cues

The tail is used for balance, and it also acts as a mood barometer. When it's held loosely upright while the cat is walking, it signals confidence. A tail that flicks toward you means "hello, my friend." Whipping the tail from side to side or thumping it on the floor signifies agitation. A lightly twitching tail conveys relaxed alertness. When the tail puffs out, it means total fright.

The nose is an important organ to cats, who constantly sniff out chemicals called pheromones, which are produced in the glands in their cheeks, between the digits of their feet, in anal sacs, and in urine. Each time a cat sniffs another cat's scent, he learns a minibio: the cat's gender, whether it is intact or neutered, its age, and its health status.

The eyes are also key. Cats can't see in total darkness, but they can see much better than we can in dim light. They also have a pair of third eyelids that unfold when needed for protection. If your cat sports dilated eyes, give him some space: He's nervous.

The ears contain more than 40 thousand nerve fibers, which allow cats to hear very high and very low frequencies. Only the horse and the porpoise have a greater frequency range. Back off from a cat that has his ears flattened against his head; he is in a defensive posture or is ready for a catfight. Ears pointed forward and slightly outward indicate relaxation.

The whiskers are used to detect space. Cats have 24 whiskers spaced in four rows on each side of the face. They're sensitive organs that are used to protect the eyes and size up the width of entries. If the whiskers clear, the entire body can slither through.

Make Your Home Fit for a Cat

Your home can also be your cat's castle — without a lot of renovation or expense. When you think about it, cats spend more time inside the house than you do. So they deserve some décor-pleasing perks.

Cater to Your Kitty

Open a drawer in your dresser as an invitation for a catnap. If you're worried about getting clothes dirty, place an old towel on top of the items.

Satisfy your cat's curiosity by letting her explore closets while you're deciding what to wear.

If your cat likes to hang around when you're in the kitchen or bathroom, let the sink faucet drip lightly so he can take a drink. Stop the drip when you exit.

Grow some potted cat grass to fulfill your cat's plant-chewing instincts. *Bonus:* Chewing on cat grass will reduce hairballs.

Install a catwalk on brackets 2 feet below the ceiling. This gives your cat a purr-fect opportunity to explore the upper strata. Make sure that the catwalk is 6 to 12 inches wide and securely attached.

Provide different-sized and -shaped kitty houses in various rooms. Try a multilevel cat structure featuring scratching areas, hanging toys, and feathers in the living room.

Strategically place some rugs on hardwood or tile floors to cushion the ground for napping cats.

Place a cat bed in a tucked-away area of the living room. The bed is your cat's refuge, but it also keeps him within sight of family activities.

Open the blinds to allow sunshine in and to give your cat a lookout point for outdoor action.

Widen narrow windowsills with plush perch extensions that attach securely to the wall under the sill.

Treat your cat to a floor-to-ceiling scratching post. Or, wrap colorful rope around a column.

Drape throw blankets or cotton sheets over sofas and recliners so that your cat can snooze without depositing a mountain of hair on your upholstery.

Keep a toy chest for all your cat's play things. Bring out a few at a time to keep your cat occupied but not overwhelmed by the selection.

Remove temptation by stashing kitchen garbage in heavy lidded containers or inside a latched cabinet.

Did you inherit Aunt Dottie's antique vase? Display it in a safe place, out of the path of a dodging, darting cat.

Place special stickers on your windows indicating the number of cats you have. These signs can alert police and firefighters in an emergency.

Make Your Home Fit for a Cat 🐾 **7**

Is There a Veterinarian in the House?

Y ou can shield your cat from disease and injury. Many problems can be treated — if they're discovered early. Observe your cat, looking for changes in appearance or behavior. What you discover could save his life.

Healthy Habits

Between vet visits, practice these simple checks. Weigh your cat weekly. Substantial shifts — gains *or* losses — can be a clue to an underlying problem. Record the weights and report a deviation of two or more pounds to your vet.

Give your cat a thorough head-to-tail checkup at least once a week. Don't forget to check his eyes, ears, and mouth. Your observations may help catch a disease during its early stages.

Cats detest taking pills, but you can make the medicine go down easier. Insert the pill into a ball of moist cat food and give it to your cat as a treat. Follow this with a soft treat to make sure that your cat swallowed the pill.

If your cat keeps spitting out the pill, try plan B: Open your cat's jaws wide and pop the pill on top of his tongue as far back as possible. Then hold his jaws closed and massage his throat to induce swallowing. Try blowing a quick puff of air into his face. When he blinks, he also swallows.

Never give your cat an aspirin; her physiology can't tolerate it. Ditto for acetaminophen. A single dose of either can kill a cat.

Here's an easy way to make liquid medicine go down without a fuss. Tilt your cat's head slightly to one side. Place a plastic dropper — don't use a glass one in case your cat bites down on it — in the side of the cat's mouth at the cheek pouch. Deliver the liquid in small, steady amounts. This pace allows your cat to swallow each time.

🐟 🐟 🐟 🐟

Is your cat fond of eating wool or other fabrics? He may be suffering from pica. This condition is defined as repeated craving for and ingestion of non-food objects. It's hard to say what causes pica, but experts theorize that cats are prone to the syndrome if they lack fiber in their diets, were prematurely weaned, or have separation anxiety and compulsive behavior. If you find a cannonball-sized hole in your sweater, have your cat examined by your vet.

🐟 🐟 🐟 🐟

Prevent inappropriate fabric chewing by cat proofing your house. Store clothing in closed closets or laundry hampers and not on the floor. Stow wool or knit blankets in closets until you're ready to use them. Drape and tuck a cotton bed sheet over the couch to prevent your cat from eating the material.

🐟 🐟 🐟 🐟

The number for the National Animal Poison Control Center is (900) 680-0000. You will be billed $45 per case to your phone bill, with no time limit. Or phone (888) 426-4435, which bills the same fee to a major credit card. The hot line is open 24 hours a day, seven days a week. When you call, provide the name of the poison your animal was exposed to; the amount of the exposure and how long ago it occurred; the species, breed, age, sex, and weight of your pet; and his symptoms. Signs of poisoning include listlessness, abdominal pain, vomiting, diarrhea, muscle tremors, lack of coordination, and fever.

The national pet emergency hot line at (888) 738-7911 will refer you to a pet clinic if your cat needs emergency care or becomes lost.

CHECKING YOUR CAT'S PULSE

Taking a pulse is easy to do and strengthens the bond with your cat through touch. Recognize that the smaller the cat, the faster the pulse. A normal resting heart rate for a small cat ranges from 140 to 160 beats per minute; for a medium cat, from 120 to 140; and for a large cat, from 60 to 80. Determine your cat's pulse by following these easy steps:

1. Position your cat on his side.
2. Gently slide your hand under the top back leg.
3. Feel for the crease where the body meets the leg.
4. Place your first two fingers along the little groove where the artery is located.
5. Count the pulse for 1 minute. Or take a 20-second pulse and multiply by 3.

Meow-ve-lous Meals

Sure, you want to feed to please, but don't go overboard. If you truly want to pamper your cat at chow time, feed him the right amount of the right food. That's easier said than done. When a pair of gold or green soulful eyes is aimed your way, it's human nature to heap on the helpings. But resist and your cat will live a longer, healthier, and happier life.

Chow-Time Tips

Feed your cat in a room other than the dining room while you're enjoying your dinner. This prevents begging and allows you both to dine without interruption.

Switch to healthy treats, such as raw tuna cubes, instead of high-calorie store-bought treats.

Keep a schedule. Cats are habitual creatures who enjoy eating at regular intervals. Serve meals at the same time and in the same place every day.

Offer a variety of dry foods and flavors to please your kitty's palate. Switch from bags of chicken to tuna to other flavors.

Keep your cat cool and occupied during warm days by putting a few ice cubes in his water bowl.

Mealtime can also assist with some minor medical conditions. Give kitty dandruff the brush-off by adding a teaspoon of corn, safflower, peanut, or sunflower oil to your cat's main meal of the day.

Never buy low-fat cat food. Fat helps keep your cat's coat and skin healthy and gives him energy. The only issue with fat is that you shouldn't give too much.

Check the expiration date on the label and never serve your cat food that is past its prime.

Get rid of any wet food your cat leaves in his bowl after eating. Wash the bowl in hot, soapy water to prevent the growth of bacteria, such as *E. coli* or salmonella.

🐟 🐟 🐟 🐟

Buy cat food containing these nutrients: vitamin E, beta-carotene, gamma linolenic acid, omega-3 fatty acids, protein, L-carnitines, glucosamines, fiber, and chondroitin sulfates. They help repair cartilage, rejuvenate dry skin, build muscle tissue, boost the immune system, and aid digestion.

🐟 🐟 🐟 🐟

Did you know that small cats burn more calories than large cats, ounce for ounce? Or that older, less active cats need fewer calories, while growing, active cats burn more calories than couch-lounging cats? Factor in your cat's age, weight, activity level, flavor preferences, and health when selecting commercial cat food.

🐟 🐟 🐟 🐟

You hate dirty dishes — well, so does your cat! Once a week, put your cat's food and water bowls in the dishwasher for thorough cleaning.

🐟 🐟 🐟 🐟

Don't serve food or water in plastic bowls. Chew-prone cats can perforate the edges and invite bacteria to harbor and thrive. Better choices are stainless steel, glazed ceramic, or stoneware bowls.

Cats detest messes. Keep bits of food from flying everywhere by placing food bowls on vinyl place mats that can be wiped clean with a sponge.

Serve food and water at your cat's eye level. Elevate bowls so that your cat won't strain her neck and back muscles. This placement will help your cat's digestion, too.

Buy only a month's worth of dry food. Otherwise, you run the risk of the food becoming stale, rancid, or bug infested.

Go easy on cheese treats. Cheese is a great calcium source, but too much can cause diarrhea.

Label and date leftover portions of wet food and store them in sealed containers in the refrigerator for up to four days.

LEARN TO READ LABELS

Read the cat food label to determine the percentages of protein, fat, and fiber. Choose food sanctioned by the American Association of Feed Control Officials (AAFCO). The AAFCO seal indicates that the product has passed its rigorous feeding trials for balanced nutrition.

6

Safety Rules

Cats are valuable members of the family. Just as we do our best to look out for our children, we need to practice the same safety precautions for our faithful, fun-loving cats.

Be Aware

Resist the temptation to share some of your chocolate chip cookies with your cat. Chocolate contains theobromine, a stimulant related to caffeine that can cause a dangerous reaction in cats.

Treat your cat like a toddler. Both are naturally curious and need your guidance to keep them out of harm's way.

Store cleaning supplies and other kitty hazards inside cabinets with childproof latches.

As for milk, shy away from serving it, especially to kittens. Their immature digestive systems can't always digest the nutrients in cow's milk.

Wipe up and flush away any automotive spills immediately. Keep your cats indoors when changing antifreeze. Bring used antifreeze to recycling centers for proper disposal.

Provide your cat with a breakaway collar so she doesn't strangle if it gets caught on something.

Keep poisonous houseplants safely out of your cat's reach by hanging them on ceiling hooks. Cats can get sick, and even die, from eating these plants: azalea, daffodil bulbs, dieffenbachia, geraniums, holly, impatiens, ivy, mistletoe, morning glories, oleander, philodendron, and poinsettia. For a complete list, click on the Humane Society of the United States' Web site at www.hsus.org.

Elevate your shampoo, conditioner, soap, and razor out of paw and nose reach in your shower.

🐟 🐟 🐟 🐟

Never leave dental floss in an uncovered waste-basket. If curiosity prevails, your cat could ingest it and possibly choke to death.

🐟 🐟 🐟 🐟

Keep the toilet lid down to prevent your cat from using it as an auxiliary drinking bowl. The water may look clean, but it can harbor bacteria.

🐟 🐟 🐟 🐟

Use safety electrical cords that prevent shocks or sparks if gnawed on. Spritz electrical cords with Bitter Apple spray to discourage chewing.

🐟 🐟 🐟 🐟

Tack electrical wires to the floor or baseboards (just don't insert a tack directly into a wire) to keep them out of sight — and mind.

🐟 🐟 🐟 🐟

Don't use antifreeze that contains ethylene glycol (EG); it tastes sweet but is deadly to cats. It may drip from a leaky hose or radiator or spill during coolant changes. Just two ounces can kill a cat. Once swallowed, EG rapidly crystallizes and attacks the kidneys. If you suspect that your cat has ingested toxic antifreeze from a vehicle leak, call your vet immediately because there are no symptoms at first. Avoid this situation by switching to antifreeze that contains pylene glycol (PG); it performs just as well as conventional antifreeze and is essentially nontoxic to pets. It is also environmentally friendly, since it's biodegradable and contains no phosphates.

🐟 🐟 🐟 🐟

Quit smoking. Secondhand smoke bothers cats, too. In fact, one in five cats suffers from some type of allergy, including allergy to smoke.

🐟 🐟 🐟 🐟

Don't leave a pin or needle on a table after sewing. Ditto for thumbtacks and earrings. Cats are drawn to shiny objects and could injure themselves or accidentally swallow these items. Stash rubber bands, buttons, and other small items in drawers or containers.

🐟 🐟 🐟 🐟

It may sound silly, but eye the inside of your washer and dryer before adding loads of laundry. Cats are curious creatures who like dark, out-of-the-way places. They might just pop into a washer or dryer if you're not looking.

🐟 🐟 🐟 🐟

Test all window screens for firmness before raising them to let in a breeze. Cats are drawn to windowsills. They could accidentally fall out the window if the screen is not taut and secure.

Paw Laws

Where there's a will, there's a way of life for your cat . . . long after you're gone. Talk to an attorney about setting up a legal will, which protects your cat if you happen to pass away before she does.

Caring for the Long Haul

Establish a trust that designates someone to care for your cat and provides the finances for lifelong care after you die. You can designate a specific amount to be spent monthly or annually or just leave it up to the executor's discretion. You can also specify that any unused balance of the trust be donated to a Humane Society, animal shelter, or favorite animal charity. Legal trusts cost $75 to $400.

The Humane Society of the United States offers a free brochure, "Planning for Your Pet's Future Without You." It outlines steps to ensure that your cat will be cared for in a safe, loving environment after you die. Obtain the brochure by calling the HSUS at (202) 452-1100, or write their Planned Giving Department at 2100 L Street NW, Washington, D.C. 20037.

If your dear old, ailing Aunt Alice passed away and left a sweet-hearted cat behind, consider pairing him with another ailing or elderly person if you can't adopt him. Check with your local Humane Society or American Association of Retired Persons to try to place the cat in a new home. Cats who have spent time living with people in poor health are often blessed with the temperament to help another such person.

Take steps to keep your cat a law-abiding feline citizen. Check with your health department about licensing rules that apply in your community. There may be particular laws regarding the wearing of identification tags and housing limits or restrictions.

Finding a Lost Cat

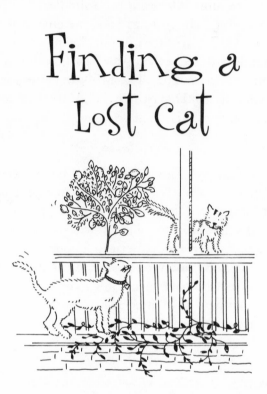

It can be a cat owner's worst fear: Your cat slips out the door and — poof — disappears. Accidents do happen occasionally, which is why you need to act now to prevent problems later.

Let's See Some ID

Always keep a collar on your cat. Attach an identification tag that, at the least, provides his name and your phone number. Use the front and back of the tag for your address and your vet's phone number. The more information, the better.

🐟 🐟 🐟 🐟

Does your cat detest collars? Gain peace of mind by having your vet surgically implant a microchip under your cat's skin that provides identification information. More and more shelters are now able to wave special detection wands over rescued cats to check for the presence of a microchip.

🐟 🐟 🐟 🐟

Update ID tags each time you move. Your best bet is to buy new tags before you arrive at your new destination, preferably the same day you fill out a change-of-address form with the U.S. Postal Service.

🐟 🐟 🐟 🐟

Keep current photos of your cats mounted on the refrigerator door. If your cat is ever lost, you can easily grab this photo to show to neighbors.

WHAT TO DO FOR MULTICAT HOUSEHOLDS

If you have more than one cat, you need to take the same precautions with each of them. To make identification easier, splurge on differently designed collars. Match each cat with a color or pattern that shows off his or her personality and highlights his or her markings. Of course, don't forget to add ID tags to each collar.

The Ins and Outs of Kitty Doors

Free yourself from doorman duty! Give your well-behaved cat some freedom of movement by installing a kitty door. These handy doors permit your cat to enter rooms that are off-limits to dogs. Cat-door kits are available through pet stores, and they're easy to install.

Happy Trails

There are many door designs suited to all types of home construction. They can be installed in existing doors or walls or set up as separate panels that act as extensions of sliding glass doors.

The door of choice should be slightly taller and wider than your cat. Select one that suits your climate, too. A plastic flap door works well in mild climates but won't protect your family from extremely cold or warm weather. If you use a plastic flap, protect your cat's welfare by making sure it is flexible, safe, and nontoxic.

Figure out which locking system works best for you and your cat. There are magnetic locks, latching locks, and electronic locks. Your cat can be fitted with an electronic device in the collar that permits only him to enter or leave the house. This prevents the occasional neighborhood cat from casually stopping over for an unannounced visit.

While you're teaching your cat how to enter and exit, add some flavor to the training session with tiny pieces of treats. Limit training sessions to no more than 20 minutes.

Build up your cat's confidence by removing the flap or door at first. Have someone stay inside with your cat while you go outside. Call your cat to come through the hole, and praise him lavishly and give him a treat when he does. Once he has the hang of it, add the door and follow the same steps.

Pet-i-cure, Please

Long nails are definitely not in fashion in the cat world. Treat your cat to regular pedicures and she will avoid snags in the carpet, infections, injuries, and scratching you.

Painless Clipping Techniques

Touch, tickle, and massage your cat's feet daily. This gets her used to having her paws handled and reduces her anxiety when you clip her nails.

Make clipping a happy event by beginning manicures when your cat is a kitten. Do it in a quiet, confined place like the bathroom to eliminate distractions — or escape routes. Close the door and wrap your cat in a thick towel for better control.

Speak in a calm, reassuring tone during the clipping. Cut only one nail the first time and gradually, as your cat keeps her cool, work your way up to all the nails on one paw. When she's ready, clip all four feet. Always finish trimming tasks with praise and treats. Your cat will soon look forward to the sight of the nail clippers because she anticipates the big payoff at the end.

Buy clippers at a pet store. These devices are specifically designed for cats, and they do the job better and safer than the human clippers you use.

If your cat has clear nails, trim just before the red "quick" area, the part of the nail that contains blood vessels. If your cat has dark nails and you can't see the quick, clip just the tip every two weeks.

Keep a styptic pencil within reach in case you accidentally cut too deeply and cause bleeding. If you're temporarily out of a styptic product, sprinkle cornstarch on the injured paw. Call your vet if the bleeding is prolonged.

Kitty Karma

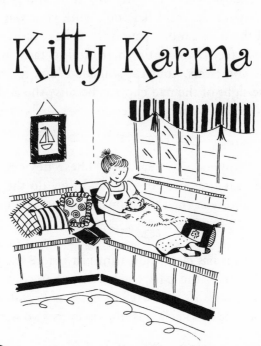

Okay, there's no scientific evidence to suggest that cats can cosmically predict next week's winning Lotto numbers. And it's well known that cats prefer rolling Ping-Pong balls to crystal balls. But there are ways to tap into the spiritual side of a feline friend from your past or present.

Keep in Touch

Talk to a pet psychic to learn how your dearly departed cat is doing in kitty heaven. He may even offer you words of advice from the great beyond. Arrange for a few friends to bring photos of their late-but-great cats to a group session with a pet psychic.

❧　❧　❧　❧

Contact a pet psychic or animal communicator to help you learn your cat's likes and dislikes and how you can improve his home life. Tune into your pet's psyche. Maybe he's jealous of the other family cat, or hates chicken, or wants you to keep the *Animal Planet* channel permanently on the television.

❧　❧　❧　❧

Meditate together. Pick a quiet time in a quiet room (turn off the telephone and television). Have your cat sit or lie next to you. Close your eyes and silently think of happy memories you share together. Clear your head of other distractions and focus only on your relationship with your cat. Start with five minutes and gradually work up to 20 minutes.

❧　❧　❧　❧

Venture into the world of Petstrology. Find out your cat's sign from a pet-oriented astrologist. Is your calico catty because he's born under the sign of Taurus? Or is your brown tabby easygoing because she's a Libra?

❧　❧　❧　❧

Respect your cat's potential ESP abilities. Some cats have been credited with predicting earthquakes and hurricanes. They become excited, restless, or fearful right before a natural disaster strikes. Listen to what your cat is telling you.

ReSpect Your Elder cats

Treat your aging cat like a CEO: Cat Extraordinaire. Your cat has been loyal to you since kittenhood. Now is the time to increase her daily dose of pampering.

Creature Comforts

Place water bowls in different locations inside the house. Older cats tend to drink less, but with water readily available, your cat is less likely to become dehydrated. Measure the water levels in the morning and again at night to determine how much your cat is drinking.

Respect your cat's periodic wish to behave like Greta Garbo. If your cat isn't in a social mood, let her have her own space.

≈ ≈ ≈ ≈

Treat your cat to a chewable pet vitamin, which provides vital nutrients that your aging cat needs.

≈ ≈ ≈ ≈

Old cats require more protein than young cats in order to maintain lean body mass and a strong immune system. Choose a food with a higher percentage of protein, or one formulated for aged cats.

≈ ≈ ≈ ≈

Continue daily exercise. Senior cats still possess a kitten's desire to play. Just go slower with the mouse or pole-chase toy and shorten playtime.

≈ ≈ ≈ ≈

On or around your cat's seventh birthday, schedule a comprehensive veterinary checkup that includes blood and urine samples. The lab-analyzed results will provide a baseline of your cat's condition and help your vet customize her care.

≈ ≈ ≈ ≈

For an arthritic cat, provide glucosamine capsules to improve mobility and joint lubrication in arthritic limbs. Ask your vet for dosage information.

≈ ≈ ≈ ≈

Keep your cat's sleeping area warm and cozy. Apply heat to an arthritic joint with a warm towel.

Be Down in the Mouth

Does your cat have doggie breath? That odious odor could be a warning sign of dental problems. According to the American Veterinary Dental Society, 80 percent of cats lacking dental care develop gum and teeth problems by age three.

Care for Pearly Whites

Look inside your cat's mouth twice a week and check for signs of deterioration, bleeding or pale gums, persistent foul breath, tartar buildup, decay, or broken or missing teeth.

Make dental care fun. Feed your cat tiny cubes of raw fresh tuna to scrub plaque away.

Choose cat-pleasing toothpaste. You may like a minty taste, but your cat prefers chicken, beef, or liver flavors. Make sure it contains chlorehexidine, which controls bacteria and fights gum infections.

Make teeth brushing a bonding time. Praise your cat as you act as her at-home dental hygienist.

For cats not yet accustomed to having fingers poked inside their mouths, build up trust by first dipping your finger into beef bouillon and then rubbing your finger gently over your cat's teeth.

Once your cat is used to the above routine, add gauze over your finger and gently scrub her teeth in a circular motion. Then, introduce a soft toothbrush designed for cats. A toothbrush massages your cat's gums and removes excess plaque.

Gently lift your cat's lip and clean his outside upper teeth where you're likely to find tartar. Work on one side of your cat's mouth at a time. Pay attention to the crevices where gums and teeth meet; this is where infections and odors may form.

Schedule a yearly professional cleaning to get rid of stubborn tartar and repair tooth damage.

14

Take the Fright Out of Vet Visits

Cats don't usually beg to see the veterinarian. The car ride alone is enough to send them into a hiss-y fit. But deep down, they know vets are necessary evils that keep them healthy and happy. Do your part by selecting a vet who caters to your cat's needs.

Choose Your Vet Wisely

Word of mouth is a terrific way to locate a skillful veterinarian. Ask pet-owning neighbors, friends, and co-workers for recommendations.

You can also contact the American Animal Hospital Association (AAHA) in Denver, Colorado for help. This professional organization promotes standards for pet care and maintains a membership of more than 12 thousand licensed veterinarians. Call AAHA's toll-free number at 800-252-2242 or visit the Web site (www.aahanet.org) for assistance.

If possible, tour the veterinary clinic before booking your first appointment. High-quality clinics will gladly guide you through their facilities and answer your questions. Look for cleanliness in the waiting room, exam rooms, labs, and kennel areas. Find out whether the clinic has evening and weekend hours and what you can do if your cat has an emergency after hours. Ask about continuing education classes and specialties that the veterinary staff may have.

How to Get There in One Piece

About an hour before the vet visit, stash the pet carrier and leash in a small room, such as a bathroom. Shut bedroom doors and other rooms with an excess of hiding places for your vet-phobic cat.

Be calm and speak in reassuring tones when you're ready to round up your cat for the vet visit.

For cats that fight being placed in carriers, try tipping the carrier so that the door is on top and open. Then pick up your cat by the scruff of his neck with his legs dangling and guide his hind legs down into the carrier. Gently ease him into the carrier and shut the door. Lower the underside of the carrier to the floor very slowly, giving your cat a chance to reposition himself.

Treat your cat to a practice run when introducing her to a new cat doc. Bring the cat to the vet's office. Let her investigate the clinic and meet the vet without being poked or prodded.

LISTEN TO YOUR VET!

Be a good cat caregiver by following your vet's advice. You'll optimize your cat's health, happiness, and longevity. In addition, have your vet perform yearly blood, urine, and other lab tests on cats over age seven to pinpoint any dietary deficiencies or early signs of diabetes, cancer, kidney problems, or other medical conditions.

15

There's the Rub!

Cats are born yoga masters; they know instinctively how to stretch properly. Stretching reduces muscle tension and stiffness, improves blood and lymph circulation, and enhances flexibility and range of motion. My friend C. Sue Furman, Ph.D., a feline massage instructor and professor of anatomy and neurobiology at Colorado State University, Ft. Collins, Colorado, highly recommends that cat owners learn how to treat their cats to regular sessions of passive stretching to promote range of motion.

Giving a Rubdown

1. Place your cat on her side on the carpet or a cushion in a quiet place that is free of distractions.

2. Hold her front leg above and below the elbow for optimal support.

3. Stretch her front leg toward her head slowly. Hold the limb for 5 seconds.

4. Stretch her front leg toward her tail. Stop at the point of resistance and hold for 5 seconds.

5. Work the other front leg in the same sequence; repeat with each of the back legs.

6. Gradually, over a period of a few weeks, increase the holding time to 10 to 15 seconds. If your cat seems uncomfortable at any time, reduce the pressure and the amount of holding time.

Dos and Don'ts

Once you've spoiled your cat with stretching, you're ready to become her personal masseuse. Massage is a hot trend among cat lovers who realize the medical, bonding, and behavioral benefits in providing therapeutic touch for their felines.

- Do approach your cat slowly and speak in a soothing tone.
- Do let your cat pick the time and place.
- Do use clean hands that are free of oils, creams, or lotions.
- Do look for lumps, cuts, fleas, or ticks.
- Do stroke the muscles in the direction of the heart to enhance healthy blood flow.

🐈 Do pay attention to your cat's feedback signs. If he hangs around, gives you a sleepy glance, or even falls asleep, you've got the right touch. If he starts wiggling, resisting, and trying to escape, end the session.

🐈 Do enroll in a feline massage class. The best instructors are licensed massage therapists who have taken additional certification courses in cat massage.

🐈 Don't massage with your feet — no matter how talented your toes are!

🐈 Don't press too deeply.

🐈 Don't give a massage when you're feeling stressed or harried. Cats read your body cues.

🐈 Don't directly massage an open wound or the site of recent surgery. Instead, *gently* massage above and below the area to stimulate blood and nutrient flow.

MAGIC MASSAGE MOTIONS

Circling. Move your fingers in small clockwise or counterclockwise circles.

Flicking. Pretend that you are lightly brushing imaginary crumbs off a table and you've got the idea behind this motion.

Gliding. Make flowing, continuous motions from head to tail.

Kneading. Flick your palm and all five fingers to gently caress the spinal area.

Rubbing. Move along your cat's body slowly, exerting feather-light, light, and mild pressures.

There's the Rub! 🐾 39

16

Catnaps and Nocturnal Romps

C ats reign as snooze kings. They typically spend 70 percent of the day sleeping. These nocturnal creatures can also be unruly at night.

How many of us have nudged, even shoved, a snoring spouse, but endured many a restless night rather than touch a single hair on our bed-hogging cat? Cats in dreamland capture our hearts.

Sweet Dreams

Try to sleep in the same position or spot all night so you won't annoy your sleeping cats. If you need to shift positions, do it slowly and gently.

Put off making the bed until your cat wakes up.

Place large pillows on hard floors to make them cushy and comfy for afternoon siestas.

Warm a blanket in the dryer and drape it on your cat during chilly nights to help her fall asleep.

Let sleeping cats enter dream cycles undisturbed.

When you're ready to awaken your cat, whisper his name. Allow his eyes to open before you touch his body so you don't startle him.

Curb sleep-disturbing nighttime play by outfoxing your feline. Change her feeding time from early morning to right before bed. A full belly helps a cat snooze longer through the night.

Spend 20 minutes or so before bedtime playing with your cat so he will be ready to go to sleep when you are.

Gently awaken your slumbering cat periodically during the day and engage her in spirited play to tire her out. She'll sleep longer through the night.

17

Kitten Antics

As cuddly cute as kittens are, they must be taught how to socialize. The prime learning time is between 4 and 14 weeks old. This is your golden opportunity to instill good manners, self-confidence, and trust in your newest addition to the family.

During this time, expose your impressionable kitten to big cats, little cats, happy cats, and playful cats. Your kitten should also meet tall people, short people, young people, old people, people with accents, and those who wear hats. And yes, even d-o-g-s!

Getting Acquainted

In addition to receiving introductions to other animals, your kitten needs to get used to her surroundings so that she doesn't develop unfounded phobias. Let her get used to the sounds of the vacuum cleaner, dishwasher, dryer, and lawn mower. Introduce her to her own reflection in mirrors. Place her on different surfaces and heights with your careful supervision. Hoist her up on the slick clothes dryer top (the surface simulates a veterinary clinic's exam table), and then let her paw through plush carpeting.

Snuff out biting habits. Kittens can get overstimulated during play and may start biting your hands. You need to teach your kitten self-control. Shake a can of pennies if he becomes nip-happy. Reward good, quiet behavior with calm petting or a treat. Your kitten will soon learn that he reaps better dividends for good behavior.

Redirect play-stalking behavior by rolling Ping-Pong balls down the hall. Kittens can't resist the chance to chase this "prey" throughout the house.

Gently handle your kitten and avoid rough-housing. If you don't, your kitten will develop aggressive tendencies that will be harder to stop when she is an adult.

Cradle your kitten instead of carrying her to prevent the squirming youngster from falling. Use both hands to pick her up. Place one hand under her chest just behind her forelegs. Put your other hand under her belly. Cradle her hind legs in one arm and let her forelegs rest on your other arm for comfort and safety.

$\approx$ $\approx$ $\approx$ $\approx$

Make your hand a friend to your kitten. Never hit your kitten or he will learn to mistrust hands and may become fear-aggressive.

$\approx$ $\approx$ $\approx$ $\approx$

Avoid long, drawn-out goodbyes. About five minutes before leaving home, give your kitten something to play with, such as a toy mouse. Walk out the door without saying a word. Don't make a big to-do when you return home or you can cause your kitten to develop separation anxiety, which may make her hyperactive and destructive.

$\approx$ $\approx$ $\approx$ $\approx$

Use this impressionable time to teach your kitten some doglike tricks and skills. Yes, a new kitten can be trained to walk on a leash. Once you're both in stride, you can walk out to the mailbox together to fetch the mail.

$\approx$ $\approx$ $\approx$ $\approx$

Train your kitten to bat a Ping-Pong ball back to you. Reinforce this behavior daily and reward with treats and praise.

18

Splish, Splash — Fluffy's Taking a Bath

Few cats sit patiently at the bathroom door with a towel draped around their necks and tail tapping in anticipation of a bath. But you can make a bath a splashing good time.

Rub-a-Dub-Dub

Shut the bathroom door. Cat-knowledgeable veterinarians tell me that cats size up a situation pretty quickly. They will wiggle, squirm, howl, and claw their way to escape if they see any opportunity — like an open door. But once they realize the door is firmly shut and they have no place to hide, they will most likely surrender.

🐟 🐟 🐟 🐟

Dress to get wet. Slip into your bathing suit or don a rubberized apron. Believe me, sooner or later you'll get the entire force of a full-body shake. If your arms will be bare, make sure your cat's nails have been clipped to avoid accidental (or intentional) scratches.

🐟 🐟 🐟 🐟

Bathroom sinks make perfect tubs for kittens and small cats. Place a towel at the bottom of the sink to keep your cat from slipping, and put supplies within easy reach. If you're treating a flea infestation, don't worry; sinks can be safely disinfected with bleach afterward.

🐟 🐟 🐟 🐟

Give your cat an old screen to grip during bath time to keep her from reaching for your skin.

🐟 🐟 🐟 🐟

If your cat loathes traditional baths, opt for a dry bath, using shampoo powder. Let the powder stay in your cat's coat for a few minutes to absorb the oil or dirt, and then brush it out.

🐟 🐟 🐟 🐟

Once your cat is wet, work from one end to the other, starting at the head. Rinse in the same order. Rinse a second time to get rid of all the soap.

Remove tar or other sticky substances with mineral oil. Then wash the area to get rid of the oil.

🐟 🐟 🐟 🐟

Put two drops of shampoo in a large jug and fill it with warm water. Pour the contents of the jug over the cat's coat before you begin wetting her down. This lets water penetrate your cat's hair coating faster. Spray on the shampoo with a spritzer bottle to coat her fur evenly.

🐟 🐟 🐟 🐟

Put cotton balls in your cat's ears before bathing her to prevent water from entering her ear canals.

🐟 🐟 🐟 🐟

Unless your cat has a skin condition that requires a special medicated shampoo, use baby or pet shampoo. Skip the human conditioners; they leave cat skin greasy.

🐟 🐟 🐟 🐟

Swathe your cat in two towels before he shakes. Finish with a third dry towel.

HELP! MY CAT STINKS!

When you can't bathe your smelly cat, sprinkle a small amount of baking soda on his coat and work it in with your fingers. Baking soda is like nature's perfume; it absorbs odors, and it isn't harmful to cats.

19

Ain't misbehavin'

No cat is perfect. For that matter, no person is, either. Don't strive for perfection in your feline pal. Instead, practice what my animal behaviorist friends call redirection. If your cat is up to mischief, call his name, then divert his attention from the misdeed by enticing him with a more appropriate — and cat-pleasing — action.

Learn the Golden Rules

1. Cats don't understand the word "no" — or, at least, they choose to ignore it.

2. Find the cause of the mischief. Only then can you take the appropriate steps to improve your cat's behavior.

3. Never physically punish your cat. If she is anxious to begin with, physical punishment will only worsen the situation. In your cat's mind, you are her true friend, so why on earth are you turning against her?

4. Distract and divert. Stop giving attention to bad behavior. Instead, give "bonuses" for good behavior.

Tricks of the Trade

If your cat scratches the arm of the chair, this behavior is reinforced each time you rush in and scream at her. Try this tactic: Apply double-sided sticky tape, heavy plastic, or aluminum foil to the chair's fabric. Provide a tall, sturdy scratching post that won't tip over near the chair. The cat will find the scratching post far more appealing.

Got a cat that attempts to bolt outside each time you open the door — usually when you have your arms full of groceries? Take away the temptation by installing a screen door in front of your regular door to minimize the chance of escape.

Prevent your furry friend from turning into a cat burglar. Store loose change in narrow-necked bottles. Stash earrings, rings, cuff links, and necklaces in fastened jewelry boxes out of paw's reach. These strategies can prevent accidental choking.

Looking for a missing earring or ring? Think like your cat. Some favorite hiding places include under the living room couch, inside shoes, under the bed, and in the dark corner of a closet.

Dissuade your cat from munching on houseplants by diverting him with his own patch of super-healthy kitty grass. When you catch your cat in the act of eating houseplants, loudly shake a can of pennies from across the room. Then take him to his patch of kitty grass and pet and praise him to encourage him to munch there instead.

For cats that like to eliminate in houseplant dirt, take away the opportunity by placing aluminum foil over the dirt.

Make kitchen counters less desirable by placing double-sided sticky tape on them. Or fill a cookie sheet with water and place it on the counter as a booby trap. Satisfy your cat's need for lofty perches with a few cat-friendly high shelves or a floor-to-ceiling platform scratching post.

What do you do with a yowling cat? Reward silence. Ignore excessive whining and crying. Cats are master manipulators. If you shout or rush up to them every time they go on a talking spree, they quickly realize this is a great ploy for attention. Instead, praise your cat warmly when he does his best mime impression and stops crying. Give him a few scratches behind the ear or a small treat.

You can stop a vocalizing cat in midmeow with just a few "common cents." Put a few pennies into a rinsed soda can. Seal the opening with some tape. Duct tape is a sturdy choice. The next time your cat goes on a chatting spree, say, "Hush" and give the can a few vigorous shakes. The noise should startle the cat enough to silence him.

Your new kitten melts your heart — and frays your telephone cords. This need to gnaw escalates during the teething phase of kittenhood. Save your electrical cords by coating them in Bitter Apple spray (available at pet stores).

Instead of constantly trying to shoo your cat off your furniture, reach a compromise. Protect your furniture with a washable throw blanket or cotton sheet that you can remove once you return home.

20

Paws-itively Fun Indoor Games

You can be a good owner by buying a wide assortment of toys for your cat. But you become a great owner when you also play with your cat. Interaction shows your feline friend that it is worth it to wake up from a catnap for playtime.

Games Cats Play

Let the Good Times Roll . . . with a remote-controlled mouse. The mouse moves across the floor, changing directions as you deem. This sparks the predator instinct in your cat.

Hide and Seek. Have your cat heel by your side in a room. Throw a small treat across the room. As the cat darts after it, slip around the corner out of sight and call his name. When he races to you, reward him with a treat and plenty of praise. Repeat four or five times.

The Predator. Hone your cat's hunting skills by attaching a toy mouse to the end of a sturdy string and flexible pole. Toss the mouse within sight of your cat. When she slinks to the ground and arches up her backside, reel in the mouse. Let the fun begin! Move the mouse up and down and side to side to give your cat a good workout while she sharpens her stalking and pouncing skills.

Flashlight Tag. Dim the lights and cast the flashlight beam on the walls and floor. Watch your cat take off in hot purr-suit!

Shake, Rattle, and Roll. Fill an empty film canister with a teaspoon of dried rice and reseal the cap with a piece of tape to prevent it from being pulled off. Your cat will enjoy hours of fun batting around this noisy toy.

21

Support the Spay Way

The birth of a litter of kittens is certainly a miracle to behold. But it's time for a reality check. There are simply not enough homes for all those kittens. Show true compassion for cats by having them spayed (for females) or neutered (for males) before six months of age.

The Benefits of Altering

If you have your female cat spayed before her first heat (estrus) cycle, you'll dramatically reduce her risk of developing uterine infections and ovarian and breast cancer.

As for the boys, neutered males experience far fewer prostate problems (including abscesses, cysts, and cancer) and can't develop the testicular cancer that occurs in unaltered males. They are less likely to roam, get into fights, demonstrate aggressiveness, or display hyperactive behavior.

SEVEN MAGNIFICENT REASONS TO SPAY OR NEUTER YOUR CAT

1. Altered cats, on average, live longer, healthier lives.

2. Female cats spayed before their first birthdays are 99.9 percent less likely to develop reproductive cancer.

3. Altered cats usually behave better.

4. You'll help stop overpopulation. One female cat and her offspring can produce more than 120,000 cats in just six years.

5. You'll help stop homelessness. Only one in four cats finds a permanent, loving home.

6. You'll stop the killings. More than 8 million surplus cats and dogs are destroyed each year because there are not enough homes for them. Taxpayers pick up the tab to the tune of $300 million.

7. It can be done early. You can spay a female or neuter a male as early as eight weeks of age thanks to improved surgical equipment and techniques and anesthesia.

Postoperative Care

Schedule the appointment early in the day so that you can pick your cat up in the early afternoon (unless your vet recommends an overnight stay; then come back early the next morning).

Select a time when you will be home for a couple of days after the surgery (such as a weekend), so that you can provide comfort and reassurance to your healing pal.

Mark your calendar for the last week in February. Each year around that time, the Doris Day Animal Foundation, based in Washington, D.C., spearheads Spay Day USA. Encourage friends to spay or neuter their kitties, or make a donation to this cause in your cat's name. Many animal shelters in the country participate during this time by offering free or discounted sterilization surgeries. For more details, you can visit the Doris Day Animal Foundation Web site at www.ddal.org.

22

Me-oWWW!
First-Aid Kits

Remember the traditional scouting motto "Be prepared?" Practice this advice when it comes to caring for your cat. You never know when she may get into a mishap that needs immediate medical attention.

To take your cat's temperature, use a human rectal thermometer or a baby thermometer. Shake it, lubricate the tip with petroleum jelly, and have someone hold your cat's front body. Lift your cat's tail and gently insert the thermometer about 1 inch. Keep it in for 1 to 2 minutes. A normal cat temperature is 101 to 102°F.

Assembling a Kit

You can purchase a ready-made first-aid kit, or you can create your own. A well-stocked kit contains:

- Cold packs
- Nonstick sterile gauze pads
- Lightweight adhesive tape that won't stick to wounds
- Cotton balls
- Cotton-tipped swabs for the ears
- Antiseptic wipes
- Tweezers
- Rectal thermometer
- Antibiotic ointment
- Hydrocortisone cream
- Diphenhydramine (such as Benadryl) capsules or tablets for bites and stings
- Styptic pencil or powder
- Phone numbers of your veterinarian and emergency pet clinic
- Mineral oil (to remove tar and other sticky substances)

BECOME A LIFESAVER

You have the first-aid kit, now take the second key step: Demonstrate just how much you love your cat by enrolling in a pet first-aid class. Contact your local Humane Society or ASPCA shelter for a class in your area. You'll learn how to perform kitty CPR and stop choking episodes, among other lessons.

23

Create a Cat-Safe Outdoors

Every indoor cat deserves fresh air. Your cat's ancestors lived outdoors, stalking mice and basking in the sunshine.

Today's outdoor world is far less kind to cats. They must contend with fast cars, cat-hating dogs, and the perils of antifreeze-stained driveways. That said, you *can* treat your cat to the sights, sounds, and smells of the great outdoors — safely.

Bringing the Outside In

Create an outdoor cat enclosure with plywood, chicken wire, and PVC pipe. These enclosures can be custom built to suit any housing situation —

from apartment balconies to kitchen window extensions.

❧ ❧ ❧ ❧

Purchase a kitty porch to attach to a windowsill. It's big enough for a cat plus water, food, and a couple of toys. Let your cat spend some time in it each day checking out the outdoors.

❧ ❧ ❧ ❧

Do you have an enclosed run for your dog in the backyard? Occasionally, let your cat take over this safe outdoor haven while you give your dog a bath with the garden hose.

❧ ❧ ❧ ❧

Train your cat to walk on a leash. Make sure the leash is attached to a cat harness to avoid any neck injuries that could occur if your cat is startled and yanks or leaps. Stick with properly fitting nylon leashes and a collar with a harness to prevent wiggling escapees.

❧ ❧ ❧ ❧

To introduce the leash and harness, casually leave them next to your cat's favorite sleeping place, food bowl, or scratching post. After a few days, put the leash and harness on your cat and let her walk around the house by herself, under your supervision. Once she has trust and confidence, you're ready to head outdoors. Never leave your cat unsupervised on a leash or chain.

24

Fat cats and Fussy Felines

Show true love by resisting the urge to overfeed your cat. We all like to indulge them, but we're slowly killing them with kindness. Each extra ounce of body fat reduces your cat's longevity, mobility, and vitality.

Fit and Trim

If you're starting to call your cat Porky Puss, do the obesity test. Place both thumbs on your cat's backbone and rub your fingers along her rib cage.

If you can't feel her ribs through the flab, she's probably overweight.

⁓ ⁓ ⁓ ⁓

Weigh your cat once a week using the same scale. Record the weight to the exact ounce on a notepad near his food containers. A weight gain of a couple of pounds on an adult cat over a month's time is your signal to cut back on the serving size and step up the exercise time. Two extra pounds on a cat is like 10 to 20 pounds on a person.

⁓ ⁓ ⁓ ⁓

Gradually reduce the amount of chow you give your overweight cat by 10 or so percent weekly. Cut back on the treats, too. These lip-smacking goodies should never account for more than 5 to 10 percent of your cat's total daily food intake.

⁓ ⁓ ⁓ ⁓

Sprinkle wheat bran on your chubby cat's bowl of wet or dry food. It's low in calories but high in fiber, which gives the cat a sense of fullness.

⁓ ⁓ ⁓ ⁓

Help a fat feline lose a few pounds by adding more dietary fiber to his meals with a tablespoon of canned pumpkin or a half-teaspoon of Metamucil. Fiber improves digestion and helps lessen the chance of constipation.

⁓ ⁓ ⁓ ⁓

For fussy feeders, try jazzing up the meal with a teaspoon or two of chicken fat.

Never feel a lick of guilt about cutting snacks by half or giving your cat half of a treat instead of a whole one.

Sprinkle a teaspoon of kelp powder on your cat's food. Or try one standardized capsule of lecithin mixed with the food. Both help speed your cat's metabolism and break down fats.

Limit your flabby feline to a 20-minute mealtime. Remove his dish when the time limit is reached. If there are any leftovers, that's a cue that you are feeding him too much.

Provide finicky eaters with a variety of textures in food. The more pungent the smell of canned food, the greater the appeal.

Microwave refrigerated canned food for 10 seconds to warm it slightly. The warmth and enhanced aroma help attract finicky eaters.

If you own a fat cat and a slender cat, install a cage with a door just big enough for the slim feline to enter an enclosure containing a food bowl during mealtimes. Or install a magnetic pet door that gives access to the chow area and place the magnetic collar on the slim cat.

Smooth Moves

Cats know days, even weeks, before the first box is packed that the household is planning a move. Cats are turf-oriented creatures who dislike change. Moving is a stressful time for you, but don't overlook the nervousness in your cat. Now more than ever he needs your reassurance that everything will be fine.

Changing Zip Codes with Ease

Contact the local Humane Society for a list of pet-friendly landlords in the area.

Keep a file on your cat with your other important documents. Stash his medical records, current photos (just in case he slips out the door), pet care booklets, pet sitter's and vet's contact information, and a list of animal organizations (they can help if an accidental escape should happen).

🐾 🐾 🐾 🐾

During a quiet moment, tell your cat about the big move. Let him know he is coming with you and that the new place offers him new sights and smells. He may not understand your words, but he will understand your excitement and loyalty.

🐾 🐾 🐾 🐾

While movers trek in and out of your home, confine your cat to one room with a big sign CAT INSIDE — DO NOT ENTER posted on the door. Provide one of your smelly t-shirts and a favorite toy for comfort.

🐾 🐾 🐾 🐾

When searching for a new place, create a sensational résumé for your cat that highlights all her terrific traits. Indicate that she is up-to-date on all vet visits, and include letters of reference from your vet, current landlord, and neighbors.

🐾 🐾 🐾 🐾

Rub a slightly damp towel on your cat's back and then rub it on the walls, floors, and furniture inside the new home. When your cat recognizes his own scent, he will be less anxious.

If you're making a crosstown move and have access to the new place in advance, bring items that smell of the new home and place them where your cat currently sleeps and eats. This establishes a positive association with the soon-to-be-new home and helps your cat get used to the scent.

Once you move to the new location, treat your cat to a stylish new collar and ID tag with your new contact information.

Re-create a special spot in the new house that mirrors a favorite place from the old house to make your cat feel more at home. If you always had your cat's food and water bowls near the refrigerator, attempt to do the same in the new place. The same goes for selecting the location for her litter box.

Place your sweatshirt in your cat's bed at the new place so he can savor the smell of security.

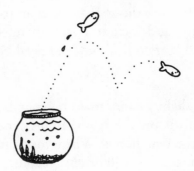

26

Get Your cat a Pet

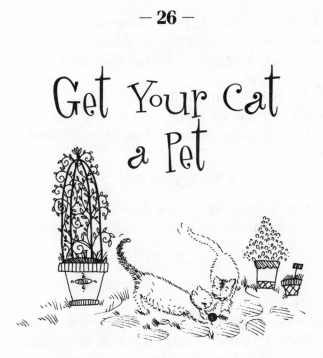

Most cats won't admit it, but they like being in the company of their peers. If you're away a lot or sense that your cat is tired of being a solo act, pair her up with a furry playmate.

Friends Forever

Your first choice should be a kitten, preferably of the opposite sex. But great friendships have been formed between two adult cats, two cats of the same sex, and cats and members of other species, such as dogs, guinea pigs, birds, and rabbits.

If your cat has strong predator instincts, don't pair her up with rodents, birds, or rabbits.

Try to pair complementary personalities. If your cat is bold and outgoing, try matching her with a cat that is easygoing and willing to be a follower, not a leader.

Bribe your cat with a new scratching post so she can associate the gift with an impending change.

Remember that some friendships form in nanoseconds and others can take weeks, even months. As long as the two aren't harming each other with bloody feuds, you need to let them work out who's boss.

To prevent any displays of selfishness, buy cat trees with multiple platforms so there is plenty of space to roost.

Remember to provide one litter box per cat in the house. If you have three cats, strategically place three litter boxes in the house. Scoop all of them daily.

Getting to Know You

Here are some ways to ensure a proper introduction without a lot of hissing or flying fur.

1. Before you pick up your new kitten, cat, puppy, or dog, set up temporary housing for him in a small, enclosed room, ideally a bathroom. Place food and water bowls on the floor and put a litter box or newspaper in the opposite corner. Provide a blanket for napping and a thick towel in the sink for an elevated bed. Close the door and go get your new pet.

2. When you enter, keep the new pet concealed under your coat or inside a pet carrier. Don't pussyfoot around. Take the new pet directly to the prepared bathroom. The goal here is to not let your house cat know that it was *you* who brought in this interloper; he may blame you by destroying your favorite sweater or purposely missing the litter box.

3. Sideline your involvement, giving your cat and the new arrival time to get to know each other. For the first introduction, allow them to sniff each other from under the doorframe. Don't display any reaction to hissing or howling.

4. Spend one-on-one time with each pet, heaping on praise, treats, and hugs. Make sure that they each feel special.

5. After a day or two, put your first cat in the enclosed bathroom for a couple of hours while letting the new pet explore each room of the house under your supervision. This helps neutralize any turf battles.

6. Take a slightly damp towel and rub it down your new pet's body. Then rub this towel on your cat's body. You're helping to mix and mingle the two scents to reduce friction between them.

7. Okay, now comes the eye-to-eye introduction. Your first cat gets to rule by being loose. In a larger room, say a bedroom or a kitchen, place the new pet in a carrier or on a leash and allow your cat time to approach and sniff.

8. Use positive reinforcement by offering bits of food each time you increase the exposure of the animals to each other. Always give a treat to your cat first, before the newcomer receives one.

9. Allow the pets to be together in the same room only when you can supervise, until you are sure that they get along.

27

Make Fleas Flee

One pair of mating fleas can produce 20 thousand offspring in just three months! A hardy species, fleas can also survive several months without a blood meal. Combine these two factors and you'll understand why your cat can become a four-legged smorgasbord for these pests.

One of the best ways to pamper your cat is to make him flea-free. You may not always be able to prevent fleas from entering your home, but you can take aggressive steps to avoid infestation.

Send the Flea Circus to Another Town

Wash your cat's collar and leash in hot soapy water once a week to get rid of flea eggs too tiny to see.

Groom your cat two or three times a week with a tiny-tined flea comb. Prepare a bowl of hot soapy water or a dish of rubbing alcohol diluted in water. Dip the comb in the solution between strokes and after the session. Either method will drown fleas; they can't swim.

Leave flea shampoo on your pet for 10 minutes for the best effect. Distract your cat by singing songs or playing some music in the bathroom. Or put a teaspoon of peanut butter on the wall facing your cat so she can lick it off while waiting.

Wash your cat's bedding and any throw rugs that reside in high pet-traffic areas once a week in hot water. Water destroys flea eggs and larvae.

Suck up fleas with a vacuum cleaner that features a beater bar. This model is powerful enough to bag adult fleas, larvae, and eggs. Then seal the bag and discard it in an outside garbage can that has a lid.

Fight back with pyrethrin. This safe, natural insecticide derived from the chrysanthemum plant kills adult fleas. Look for the ingredient — or its synthetic version, known as pyrethroid — in flea shampoos, dips, sprays, and powders. Use only those products made for cats; dog products are too strong.

Bomb them with borate. This powder kills flea larvae that have nested in the carpets and upholstery. Apply the powder once a year or every time you have your carpets professionally cleaned.

Purchase products made with nematodes through natural pet retailers or mail-order catalogs. Nematodes are wormlike microscopic organisms that infect and kill fleas naturally. Sprinkle these products on your lawn where fleas hide.

Crush a fresh clove of garlic into each of your cat's meals. This aromatic spice won't kill fleas, but it effectively acts as nature's flea repellent.

Roust them with rotenone. A natural insecticide that kills adult fleas, rotenone is derived from the *Derris ellipta* plant. Look for rotenone in shampoos, sprays, and rinses. Do not use this product on kittens or old cats.

Feed your cat a high-quality diet. My holistic veterinarian friends tell me that fleas prefer sickly cats to cats that get healthy chow and plenty of exercise.

Stash some cedar chips in the washable cover of your cat's bedding. Fleas detest the cedar smell.

Need an Acupuncture Needle?

A cupuncture is an ancient Chinese medicine based on the philosophy that disease results from an imbalance in *qi,* the body's energy. It restores energy balance through the insertion of special tiny needles strategically placed along *meridians,* or defined paths, in the skin. Meridians correspond to different areas of the body, including the head, heart, lungs, and liver.

Know the Basics

Acupuncture activates sensory receptors that control temperature, pain, and pressure, and improves circulation, muscle tone, and immunity.

⌐∞ ∞ ∞ ∞

This treatment can complement traditional veterinary care, but seek qualified professionals. Fortunately, you have terrific resources in the International Veterinary Acupuncture Society (IVAS), based in Longmont, Colorado, and the American Veterinary Medical Association (AVMA).

∞ ∞ ∞ ∞

Acupuncture treatment costs between $65 and $100 for an initial visit and from $35 to $65 for subsequent sessions, which average 30 minutes.

∞ ∞ ∞ ∞

Acupuncture is not a cure-all. It works best for chronic conditions, such as back pain, asthma, and allergies, but it is not recommended for pregnant cats or cats with high fevers.

∞ ∞ ∞ ∞

A close cousin to acupuncture is acupressure. This method uses the strategic placement of fingertips, rather than needles, along meridian points. For instance, there is a pressure point called BL60 on the outside of the rear ankle. Press this spot between your thumb and index finger for 60 seconds once or twice a day and you'll help improve blood flow for an arthritic cat.

29

Purr-fect Herbs

Your garden may aptly serve as a backyard pharmacy for what ails your cat. Herbs harbor the healing power of nature's oldest medicines. Active constituents inside a plant's flowers, petals, stems, and roots can be used to prevent or treat a variety of physical and emotional woes.

Beyond the garden, herbs also stock the shelves of supermarkets, drug stores, and health food stores in tea, tincture, and capsule forms.

Selecting the Right Remedies

Ever watch your cat chew grass? Does he like the taste? Maybe. Maybe not. Most likely he ingests grass because he instinctively knows its ingredients will help him overcome a bout of indigestion or other minor stomach malady.

As cats become full-fledged members of our families, they deserve safe, natural treatments free of side effects whenever possible. Before giving your cat herbal medicine, always check with a holistic-minded veterinarian or member of the American Herbalists Guild to determine the right herb in the right dose for your cat.

Here is a sampling of herbs for some common kitty conditions:

- **Allergies.** Chamomile, nettle, ox-eye daisy
- **Anxiety.** Passionflower, Rescue Remedy (a mixture of flower essences)
- **Arthritis.** Alfalfa, dandelion, devil's claw, parsley, yucca
- **Bleeding.** Cayenne, shepherd's purse
- **Burns and cuts, minor.** Aloe, calendula, St.-John's-wort
- **Constipation.** Plantain, senna, turmeric
- **Diarrhea.** Marsh mallow, slippery elm
- **Flatulence.** Chamomile, dill, fennel, peppermint
- **Fleas.** Chaparral, sage, wormwood
- **Hyperactivity.** Skullcap with valerian or chamomile
- **Indigestion.** Dill, hawthorn, marsh mallow, plantain, slippery elm

- 🐈 **Infections (bacterial or viral).** Cat's claw, echinacea, garlic
- 🐈 **Motion sickness.** Ginger
- 🐈 **Nervousness.** Hop, valerian
- 🐈 **Skin problems.** Burdock, ginger, sage
- 🐈 **Urinary infections.** Echinacea, marsh mallow, yarrow

A HEALTHY TREAT

Bring the outdoors inside by treating your cat to her own personal garden. Grow a little wheatgrass (available at pet stores) in the house. This nutritious grass will satisfy your cat's need to nibble on greens and may save a few houseplants.

30

Cruising With Your Kitty

If the only time your cat rides in your car is to go to the veterinary clinic, it's no wonder that he howls and dives under the bed the minute you jingle your car keys.

Ninety-nine percent of car rides should be fun for your cat. You may not be able to make him beg you to take him for a checkup, but you can try some tricks designed to make car trips a little bit easier.

Hit the Road, Jack

Hold off on feeding your cat for a few hours prior to the start of your trip. No need to increase the risk of a stomachache caused by motion sickness.

Some cats need antihistamine or motion sickness pills — prescribed by a vet — before venturing on a road trip. If your cat gets sick in the car, talk to your vet about medications.

Work your way up to long trips by first getting your cat accustomed to frequent, short trips. Start by spending 5 to 10 minutes inside the car (with the engine off). Then take a drive together around the block. Short trips also help you determine how your cat reacts inside a car and whether she is prone to motion sickness.

Never leave your cat alone inside your car during any season, but especially in the hot summer — even for a few minutes. Leaving the windows open a crack is no guarantee against heatstroke. Your cat can become severely sick, or even die.

Give your cat a flea bath before making a long trip. Neither of you would like to be itchy and scratching on the interstate.

Buckle up. Some manufacturers offer sturdy, partially open cat carriers that permit cats to take in the view without roaming loose in the car. Check pet stores for carriers that feature a quick-release snap that attaches to the cat's harness. A strong, plastic body, washable comfort pad, and adjustable nylon straps are also good features.

For long car trips, pack some frozen water bottles so your cat will have cold water to drink as the bottles thaw. Also bring some dry food stored in airtight containers.

Place your cat in a larger carrier that has space for a small litter box. But bring a smaller carrier, too. That way, you can keep your cat safe in the backup carrier while you're cleaning the litter box.

Bring a couple of bandannas during hot weather. Soak them in cold water, wring them out, and wrap them loosely around your cat's neck and back for a few minutes of cooling relief.

Store a collapsible carrier in the trunk so you will always have one handy in case you need to rush your cat to a vet or you find a stray kitty wandering the streets.

Carry water for your cat, even on short rides. A quick trip can sometimes unexpectedly become a long journey.

Pack springwater in resealable, plastic containers for long car rides. Springwater contains no additives, preservatives, or contaminants, making it the beverage of choice for your thirsty feline.

Keep a spray bottle of water within reach. On long, hot rides, spritz your cat's face and paws to cool her down.

For long trips, bring your cat's food, medication, and comfy bed and a couple of toys.

Praise your cat with a few treats and lots of kind words along the way. This puts him at ease and lets him know how much you value him for sharing the journey with you.

Serenade your cat with classic tunes from the 60s, 70s, and 80s on a golden oldies station. Who knows? He may be inspired to become your howling backup singer!

31

Making the Skies Friendlier

Airplane travel with your pet is sometimes a necessity — and one that causes great worry for most owners. Here are some ways to pilot a happy takeoff and smooth landing for your cat.

Up and Away

Schedule an appointment with your veterinarian within 10 days of the scheduled flight. Most airlines require up-to-date medical certificates verifying that your cat is healthy enough to make the trip and is current on all necessary inoculations.

Attach ID tags with your name, address, and phone number on your cat's collar. Paste the same information on the outside of the crate and keep it inside your purse or carry-on luggage.

❧   ❧   ❧   ❧

Bring a current photograph of your cat with you. If your cat gets lost in the airport or at the destination, the photo can make the search go much more smoothly.

❧   ❧   ❧   ❧

Book early. If you have a cat under 15 pounds, he may be able to ride with you in the passenger section on some airlines. Check before finalizing a reservation. Some airlines limit the number of pets per flight to two or three. Most make pet reservations on a first come, first serve basis. The crate must be able to slide easily under the seat in front of you. Acceptable onboard airline carriers are 23 inches long by 13 inches wide by 9 inches high.

❧   ❧   ❧   ❧

For cats who must travel in the baggage compartments below, invest in a secure, heavy-duty crate. The best choice is a noncollapsible crate made of aluminum or a plastic-aluminum combination.

❧   ❧   ❧   ❧

The crate should be just big enough for your cat to lie down, stand up, and turn around easily. Don't think bigger is better. Too much wiggle room and he may be chilled or injured from bouncing against the crate wall.

Store the leash in your carry-on luggage and not inside the crate. This keeps your cat from accidentally getting caught or strangled, or having the leash get lost.

Avoid putting food in the crate. The ride is upsetting for cats and can lead to digestive problems.

Put ice cubes in the water tray of the crate.

Pack some paper towels in your carry-on bag just in case a kitty accident happens.

Seek direct flights whenever possible to avoid accidental transfers or delays. Always travel on the same flight as your cat.

Consult your veterinarian about the need for tranquilizers or natural relaxing herbs for your cat.

Select the time and date of your flight on the basis of weather conditions. Avoid flying during bitter cold winters and in the middle of the day during hot summers.

Place a blanket inside the pet carrier to keep your cat from suffering chills during winter flights.

Make sure that the airplane is equipped with ventilation in class D. This is the compartment for transporting live animals and baggage. Airlines are not required to provide ventilation by law — yet.

Contact your favorite airlines and let them know you and others want to make it safe for animals to travel by air.

Go to Hawaii solo. This state requires all cats to be quarantined from 30 to 120 days at a cost of about $600 per animal. Definitely not paradise in the eyes of your cat.

BECOME AN ACTIVIST

Lobby your legislators to make the skies more friendly for your cat. The U.S. Congress recently attached the "pets on planes" amendment to the Federal Administration reauthorization bill. This bill requires airlines to report all incidents of loss, injury, or death and to provide training for airline employees on how to handle traveling pets. It also requires the retrofitting of airplane cargo areas so that they provide adequate temperature and ventilation control.

32

The Inside Scoop on Litter

The beauty of sharing your home with a cat is that you don't have to dash out on a bitter cold or rainy day so that your pet can take a potty break. But the last thing you want to hear when a newcomer steps in your door and holds his nose up in the air is "oh, you have cats."

First, give thanks to an inventive chap named Edward Lowe. Back in the late 1940s, Lowe, a Michigan clay salesman, came up with the brilliant idea of using his product as cat-box filler. Thus, kitty litter was born.

Litter has evolved into a $950 million industry, with more than 400 billion pounds produced each year. It's made from a wide assortment of ingredients, including wheat, pine, cedar, corn, mineral clay, silica, recycled newspaper, and zeolite.

Keep It Fresh

Scoop out your cat's litter deposits every day. Would you like to use a dirty toilet? Cats are like Felix of *The Odd Couple;* they like things neat.

When you change the litter, wash the box with warm, soapy water, but never ammonia. Allow the box to dry thoroughly before you add new litter.

Three inches is the ideal depth for litter in the box at all times.

Don't place the litter box next to your cat's food and water bowls. Would you enjoy eating next to a toilet? A cat's sense of smell is so much superior to ours that the odor would be paws-itively unbearable. Plus, cats instinctively won't eliminate near their food source.

Position a small oscillating fan near the litter box to ventilate the area. If you're handy, install an exhaust fan in the room.

Don't play musical chairs with the litter box. Cats are creatures of habit and don't like surprises.

$\wp$ $\wp$ $\wp$ $\wp$

Location, location, location. Think like a realtor and place the litter box in a place that has easy access day and night. And keep it far from noisy appliances, hissing radiators, or heat vents.

$\wp$ $\wp$ $\wp$ $\wp$

Big cats need big litter boxes. The tiny litter box your cat enjoyed as an itty-bitty kitty won't do once he's an adult.

$\wp$ $\wp$ $\wp$ $\wp$

Avoid using litters that are perfumed, especially with lemon or flower fragrances. Most cats hate these scents.

$\wp$ $\wp$ $\wp$ $\wp$

Don't keep a lid on the litter box unless you scoop daily and clean out the container weekly. Lids have a tendency to trap the odors inside the box, making it less inviting for cats.

$\wp$ $\wp$ $\wp$ $\wp$

Choose litters that clump, which makes it easier to keep the box free of urine and feces. Try wheat litter for allergy-sensitive cats. This biodegradable litter forms clumps that can be safely flushed down toilets.

$\wp$ $\wp$ $\wp$ $\wp$

Use shredded paper if your cat has just undergone surgery or been declawed.

33

Cat Scratch Fever

Cats love to leave their mark, and what better way to do so than by clawing up your couch? Scratching is instinctive behavior, and even declawing won't rid your cat of this need (though it will eliminate the source of the damage). Since declawing is serious surgery that can have complications, consider these strategies for helping your cat find an appropriate place to scratch.

Solutions You Both Can Live with

Place oak tree limbs in Christmas tree stands and let the cat go to town.

Check your cat's nails. Scratching intensifies when the nails are long and in need of a pedicure.

Look at what and where your cat scratches. Offer a suitable substitute in the same vicinity. If your cat likes rattan material, try to replicate it with a scratching post made with similar material.

Be the Martha Stewart of the cat world and match the color and design of the scratching posts to your living room furniture.

Sprinkle catnip on the scratching post and spray Bitter Apple (available at pet stores) on your upholstery. Your cat's nose will inevitably lead her to the preferred spot.

Customize a scratching post. Start by nailing two flat, square pieces of wood to two ends of a lumber post. The base should be big enough and heavy enough to prevent the structure from tipping over. Attach old carpet, or even corkboard, to the base and posts using a hammer and nails or a staple gun. Add finishing touches, such as bells, feathers, and balls.

As a last resort before declawing, cover your cat's razor-sharp claws with soft adhesive nail caps, which are available through pet stores and Web sites.

34

Paw-ticulars on Hotel Lodging

Practice petiquette while traveling with your feline mate. Although many hotels do not accept animals, some do. If you decide to lodge at one of those sites, make the stay a pleasant one for you and the hotel staff by following a few simple rules.

Room Service!

Always bring a portable litter box with plenty of fresh litter (and don't forget the scooper).

Bring only house-trained cats to a hotel. Just as you don't want a cat to have an accident on your carpets or furniture, neither does the hotel staff.

Don't attempt to sneak your cat in. There are many reasons for the pet ban at certain hotels, including the welfare of guests who have pet allergies.

Be sure to pack your cat's favorite blanket or bedding to make her feel more at home in an otherwise strange place.

Never allow your cat to roam freely in the room while you're out. Keep her feeling cozy inside her carrier with a favorite toy, food and water, blanket, and mini litter box.

Tip the housekeeper well; there will be a little extra work involved in de-catting the room after you depart.

Got a mouse? No, not the varmint type — the computer type! Click onto your favorite search engine and look for a listing of pet-friendly hotels.

35

Seafaring Cats

Cats make terrific sailing companions. If you've decided to retire early to live on a sailboat and cruise up and down the coast, here are some tips to keep your cat in ship-shape.

Finding Your Sea Legs

Consider getting a second cat as a companion for your friend. She'll have an easier time adjusting to her new life if she has something to occupy her interest. Make all introductions before you make the move to onboard life, however.

Make sure your cat is up-to-date on all his vaccinations. Traveling to different locations can increase his exposure to disease.

The earlier you introduce your cat to life on the seas, the better and faster he will develop his sea legs.

Don't declaw a seafaring cat. She needs all her claws to steady her balance and climb back onboard if she accidentally falls off the boat.

Keep burlap matted rugs hanging over the edges of the boat to provide needed traction. Make sure your cat knows the locations of these rugs.

Make sure the engine area is closed to prevent a dangerous investigation by your curious cat.

Use food and water bowls with nonskid bottoms to keep them from sliding around.

Provide bottled water for your cat. She may have a sensitive tummy while she adjusts to boat life.

Keep a long-handled fish net handy to scoop out a cat that suddenly finds herself doing the dog paddle in the water.

36

Get into the Spirit

Cats will concede that God spelled backwards is Dog. But our feline friends also possess a strong sense of spirituality that we are just beginning to understand. More and more folks are starting to recognize the spiritual bond they have with their cats.

Make the Connection

Mark your calendar for the first week of October and plan ahead. You can have your cat blessed by a priest at the Washington National Cathedral in the nation's capital during this week. The majestic, historic cathedral is located at the intersection of Massachusetts and Wisconsin Avenues NW.

Or head to the Big Apple. The Blessing of the Animals is performed every Christmas Eve at the Central Presbyterian Church on Park Avenue and 64th Street in New York City.

If the nation's capital and New York City are too far, check newspaper listings or contact your local Humane Society to find out details on pet blessings in your area. They are usually scheduled around Christmas (December 25) or the Feast Day of St. Francis of Assisi (October 4).

Arrange a private blessing ceremony with your friends and neighbors. Invite them to bring their cats, too.

Get in the habit of saying grace with your pet at mealtime or give thanks as you cuddle him.

Practice what you've heard preached. Work with your local animal shelters to bring adoptable cats to your church or synagogue after worship service for adoption.

Pray with your cat, offering sincere gratitude for being blessed with such a loving pal. Each day, create a prayer time that is quiet, calm, and without distractions for both of you. Balance your requests with thanks.

37

Good Toys, Bad Toys

Play brings out the kitten even in an old cat. But it's up to you to distinguish the fun, safe toys from the bad, harmful ones. Be a discerning customer when you purchase new cat toys.

Choose Wisely

The following toys top my list of paw pleasers.

Any toy made of hard rubber, vinyl, latex, or nylon passes the durability test. Your cat will enjoy these toys for months, even years.

Ping-Pong balls are lightweight, highly mobile, and inexpensive. Roll one down the hallway and watch your cat zoom into action. Or stick a ball in an empty tissue box and let your cat use her mental powers to figure out how to fish it out. Hide the balls when playtime is over or you'll hear them flying across the kitchen floor in the middle of the night.

Wads of paper are also a perennial favorite. Crumple up a piece of paper and your cat will turn into a feline version of Wayne Gretzky, showing off his hockeylike moves around table legs.

Paper grocery bags (with the handles snipped off) are irresistible. Cats just love to get in the bag.

The Sunday newspaper isn't a traditional toy, but cats love it anyway. Spread the paper on the floor and watch your cat make full-body dives on and under it. Spice up the fun by putting her favorite toy among the papers so she can pounce and hunt for it.

Empty cardboard toilet paper tubes are great fun. Send a tube rolling on the ground and watch your cat delight in joyful pursuit.

The Cat Dancer, which is available at pet stores and through catalogs, is a long wire with tight rolls of paper at the end. Wave the toy like a wand and the paper ends move unpredictably, much like a buzzing airborne fly.

Aluminum foil balls and ribbons or yarn should be used only while your cat is supervised, since they can cause intestinal blockage if swallowed. Put them away when playtime is over.

Toys to Avoid

Steer clear of these toys and materials:

- ❖ Toys with tiny parts or glued-on pieces, such as plastic eyes; these parts pose a choking hazard.
- ❖ Soft foam balls that can be easily shredded into small pieces.
- ❖ Plastic bags, especially the handled type from the supermarket. Your cat can choke on them or can get trapped inside and suffocate.
- ❖ Knotted socks or old shoes. These will only teach your cat to chew on all socks and shoes.
- ❖ Empty cigarette wrappers. The cellophane or foil wrapper can cause choking.

climatize Your cat

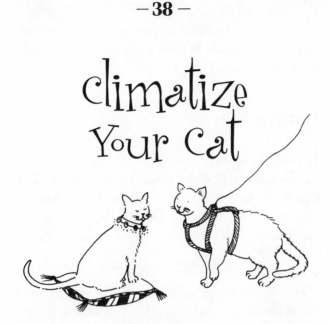

Y ou may not be able to put a leash on Mother Nature or teach her to heel, but you can buffer your cat from extreme temperatures. Extra care is needed for very young and very old kitties.

Summer Safety

Apply sunscreen around the eyes, ears, nose, and underbellies of light-colored cats to prevent sunburn.

For a leash-cooperative cat, stick to cool surfaces, such as grass under shady trees. Pick her up so that she doesn't have to walk on sizzling hot asphalt or concrete surfaces.

Go easy on exercise for your cat during humid summer days, especially if she has a short, pushed-in face. These breeds have more difficulty breathing in hot, humid weather.

Winter Wariness

If your cat escapes outside, wash her paws with a dampened warm towel once you've retrieved her. Chemical salts thrown on sidewalks to melt ice can irritate her footpads and can be poisonous if she licks the salt off her paws.

Wrap your cat in warm towels just pulled from the dryer to take the chill out of his coat quickly.

Cats that stay indoors during the dry winter months are prone to static electricity. Stop static by keeping your house at 50 percent humidity. Place a couple of humidifiers in high-traffic areas in your home.

Keep your hands well-moisturized during the winter to reduce static electricity. Ask your vet for a cat-safe conditioning rinse or spray that can help your cat's coat maintain its moisture.

catnip clues

Catnip is the caviar of cats. Botanists know it best as *Nepeta cataria,* a member of the mint family. Catnip acts as a stimulant in felines — definitely the cat's meow! Before you know it, your cat will be salivating, rolling, rubbing, and leaping. In people, catnip has just the opposite effect. It may naturally induce a blissful catnap!

'Nip Tips

Many cats react to catnip because of its active ingredient, called *nepatalactone,* which closely resembles a chemical found in the urine of female cats. This may explain why male cats seem more animated by catnip than females.

Grow a container of catnip in your outdoor garden or in a room in the house that's off-limits to your cat. The fresher, the better. Bruise the catnip leaves and stems slightly before chopping them up and serving about a teaspoonful to your cat.

If using dried catnip, store it in an airtight container in the refrigerator to extend its freshness.

Serve a teaspoon of the herb to your cat weekly. Any more and the effects diminish.

Serve catnip on a paper plate or a throw rug, or sprinkle it on a scratching post.

Jazz up playtime with toys that contain catnip.

Create homemade toys by filling a knotted piece of fabric with dried catnip. When the catnip loses its zip, empty it and refill it with a fresh helping.

Remember that catnip is best served to felines over three months of age. Younger kitties don't usually react to it, and early exposure may desensitize them.

40

Lend a Paw

If you adopted a cat from an animal shelter, that's paws-itively great! But don't make that your last visit to a shelter. Pamper homeless cats by making their shelter stays more pleasant. Each shelter has different needs and programs.

How You Can Help

If you want to continue helping, consider these acts of kindness.

Agree to be an adoption counselor. Here's your chance to be a true matchmaker. Help pair people with cats to make a good union for both.

Offer to be an animal socializer. At many shelters, a room that resembles a living room is designated as the socialization room. The goal is to have volunteers play with cats in this room to get them used to household furnishings and handling.

Become a cat foster parent. You'll provide a temporary loving home for sheltered kittens or cats to build up their socialization skills and confidence. Once they leave your home, their chances of being adopted should soar!

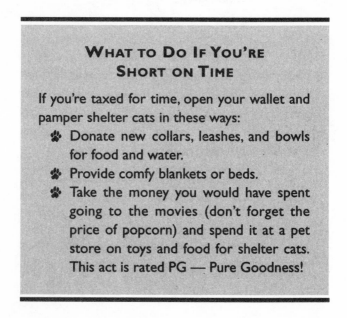

WHAT TO DO IF YOU'RE SHORT ON TIME

If you're taxed for time, open your wallet and pamper shelter cats in these ways:

- ❀ Donate new collars, leashes, and bowls for food and water.
- ❀ Provide comfy blankets or beds.
- ❀ Take the money you would have spent going to the movies (don't forget the price of popcorn) and spend it at a pet store on toys and food for shelter cats. This act is rated PG — Pure Goodness!

41

Kitty Cuisine

Want to truly win over your cat? Treat her to a Sunday feast of homemade kitty cuisine. It's easier than you might imagine and truly shows your love and affection.

As mega meat eaters, cats are true carnivores. However, diets enriched with veggies can offer added nutrition. Here are some recipes that have won over the hearts — and tummies — of some of my cat pals.

Always let food cool before serving, and refrigerate or freeze leftovers in airtight containers for up to one week.

Heavenly Kitty Hash

To vary this recipe, substitute barley for rice, flounder for ground turkey, or wheat-germ oil for corn oil. **3 servings**

  1 cup water
  ⅓ cup uncooked brown rice
  2 teaspoons corn oil
  Pinch salt
  ⅔ cup lean ground turkey
  2 tablespoons chopped liver
  1 tablespoon bone meal

1. In a medium saucepan, bring the water to a boil. Stir in the rice, corn oil, and salt and reduce the heat to low. Allow the mixture to simmer for 20 minutes, covered.

2. Add the ground turkey, chopped liver, and bone meal. Stir frequently and simmer for 20 more minutes.

Colossal Cat Chowder

Your cats will meow for more of this mouthwatering dish. **5 servings**

  ½ pound white fish, deboned and diced
    into small cubes
  1 cup creamed corn
  1 cup skim or low-fat milk
  ¼ cup red potato, finely chopped
  2 tablespoons onion, finely chopped
  1 tablespoon liver, finely chopped
  1 clove garlic, minced
  Pinch salt
  ¼ cup low-fat grated cheese

1. In a medium saucepan, combine all the ingredients except for the cheese. Cover and simmer over low heat for 20 minutes, stirring occasionally.

2. Remove from the heat and sprinkle with cheese.

Purr-fect Tuna Patties

For a simple variation on this feline-favorite recipe, sub-stitute salmon, mackerel, or whitefish for the tuna.
5 servings

2 eggs
1 6½-ounce can of water-packed tuna, drained and flaked
1 small onion, peeled and finely chopped
1 cup bread crumbs
1 teaspoon brewer's yeast
1 teaspoon bone meal
Pinch salt
2 tablespoons margarine

1. In a medium-sized bowl, whip the eggs.

2. Add the tuna, onion, bread crumbs, brewer's yeast, bone meal, and salt. Thoroughly blend with a wooden spoon until moistened.

3. In a skillet, melt the margarine over medium heat. Take small handfuls of the mixture and form 5 patties. Place the patties in the skillet. Cook each side for 3 to 5 minutes, or until golden brown.

4. Place the patties on a plate. Once they are cooled, crumble them into small pieces.

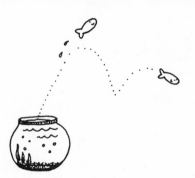

Sensational Kidney Stew

This recipe contains an aromatic mix of kitty-pleasing foods. **6 servings**

1 ½ cups water
1 tablespoon corn oil
Pinch salt
½ pound beef kidney, diced
½ cup uncooked brown rice
1 medium carrot, finely grated
4 mushrooms, finely chopped
2 tablespoons tomato paste
1 teaspoon bone meal

1. In a saucepan, combine the water, corn oil, and salt. Bring to a boil over medium heat.

2. Stir in the beef kidney, rice, carrot, mushrooms, and tomato paste and bring to a boil again.

3. Cover the saucepan, reduce the heat to low, and simmer for 20 minutes, stirring occasionally.

4. Remove from the heat and add the bone meal.

Brush Up on Your Grooming Skills

Except for the rare hairless breeds, cats shed. It's one of life's certainties. That means you should expect to find cat hair on your furniture, along the baseboards, and in the carpeting. Although cats are fastidious groomers, often spending up to 15 percent of their day cleaning their coats, they still shed.

Brushing your cat promotes a healthy shedding process, removes loose hair, stimulates the skin, and leaves your cat's coat shining.

Fur Finery

Short of shaving him, here are some tips for preventing your home from becoming a giant fur ball.

Use two-sided tape to attach plastic self-grooming combs along the lower corner of a wall. These products permit your cat to rub against the plastic bristles and get a grooming any time he desires.

❧ ❧ ❧ ❧

For the first grooming session, use a soft-bristled brush. Call your cat in a cheery tone and reward him with a small treat. Start at the tip of the fur and gently work deeper into his coat to prevent the brush from getting trapped in tangles or clumps.

❧ ❧ ❧ ❧

Always brush in the direction of your cat's coat. Going against the grain can irritate her skin and make her want to flee the scene when she sees you pulling out the grooming supplies. Use straight strokes for longhaired breeds; circular motions can break hair.

❧ ❧ ❧ ❧

Set aside five minutes each morning to brush your cat. Suck up hair that falls on the floor with a vacuum cleaner.

❧ ❧ ❧ ❧

If your cat will tolerate it, adjust the vacuum to reduce the suction (usually by sliding open the hole cover in the hose tube) and run the upholstery brush over his coat to catch the loose hair. Don't force the issue if your cat doesn't like this type of grooming.

Loosen a shedding coat by brushing while using a blow dryer. Turn the dryer to a low, cool setting to avoid burning your cat's skin.

To make cleanup easy, slip a piece of old panty-hose over the head of the brush before grooming. The bristles will poke through, and all you have to do is pull up on the pantyhose to discard the hair.

Keep brushes in various places in your house. That way, your cat can be treated to a spur-of-the-moment grooming without you having to hunt for a brush.

After a thorough brushing, treat your cat's skin and coat to a dab or two of fresh aloe to restore moisture.

Practice brush hygiene. First, remove excess hair from the brush with an old comb. Once a week, soak the brush in a sink filled with warm water and a couple of tablespoons of shampoo. Rub the soapy mixture into the bristles and let it soak for five minutes. Rinse thoroughly with warm water and add a little white vinegar to get rid of any lingering soap residue.

43

Pet Insurance

Monthly household budgets often include money for mortgages, car loans, college tuition, and health insurance premiums. But many of us cat lovers — in fact, 99 percent of us — overlook a major potential money-draining source to the household budget: medical expenses for our feline chums.

Why Get Insurance?

Only 1 percent of American pet owners have pet health insurance. That's a striking contrast to the more than 50 percent of Swedish pet owners who carry pet insurance. No one wants to be forced to make a decision based on "economic euthanasia." Cats should be put down only because it is medically necessary to relieve them of pain and suffering — not because the cost of care would hamper your budget.

◦ ◦ ◦ ◦

Pet health insurance is a money-saving way to ensure that your cat's medical needs will always be met. Premiums vary among companies as well as among cats. Typically, premiums are less expensive for kittens than for senior cats and for healthy cats than for those with diagnosed conditions, such as allergies or cancer.

◦ ◦ ◦ ◦

In most cases, the insurance covers 70 to 90 percent of expenses. Veterinary Pet Insurance, based in Anaheim, California, is the nation's largest pet health insurer. Their health plans cover office calls, prescriptions, treatment, lab fees, X rays, surgery, and chiropractic procedures performed by a licensed veterinarian. You pay the bill and then file a claim with VPI; the company reimburses you within 7 to 10 days. The policy permits you to take your insured pet to any licensed veterinarian, veterinary specialist, or animal hospital worldwide. That's peace of mind, especially if your cat travels with you. For more details, contact VPI at (800) USA-PETS (800-872-7387) or on the Web at www.petinsurance.com.

44

Picking a Pet-Pleasing Sitter

I f you're going to be away from home for two or
more days and you don't know any cat-savvy
neighbors, rely on a professional pet sitter to
cater to your cat's daily needs. The good news is
that this is a growing business, so there are bound
to be a few pet sitters in your area. For planned
trips, it's best to contact and interview a pet sitter
a couple of weeks in advance.

Stress-Free Sitter Care

Ideally, you should have the pet sitter stop by a few times and visit with your cat before you go away on a trip. This strategy helps your cat feel more comfortable with the pet sitter and reduces his anxiety level while you're gone.

Make sure the pet sitter knows your cat's likes and dislikes and what the house rules are. For instance, are couches welcome spots or off-limits to your cat? What's the limit on daily treats?

Tell the pet sitter not to remove your cat's ID collar tags at night before bedtime — just in case of accidental escape.

Make your refrigerator door Cat Information Central. Post a note that lists your cat's name and nickname; how much, what, and when she eats; the location of the food; location of and directions for any medications; leash location; and, most important, how to contact you and your veterinarian.

Introduce your pet sitter to a friendly neighbor before your departure and have them exchange phone numbers.

For local referrals, try contacting the National Association of Professional Pet Sitters (NAPPS) at (800) 296-PETS or check out their Web site, www.petsitters.org. You can also contact Pet Sitters International (PSI) at (800) 268-SITS or visit them on the Web at www.petsit.com.

YOU CAN NEVER PROVIDE ENOUGH INFORMATION

Ensure that your cat will be safe and happy while you're away by providing the pet sitter with these essentials:

- ❧ Extra cash in case the food runs out
- ❧ Directions for setting the thermostat in case of dramatic changes in the weather
- ❧ A list outlining potential pitfalls around the house ("Always close all doors very quickly because Murphy likes to try to dart outside," or "Keep the toilet lid down because Lamar is a bowl drinker.")

45

Home Alone

When you're away from home, don't expect your cat to fight boredom or anxiety by working a crossword puzzle, picking up cross-stitching, or writing the Great American Novel. Cats think and act differently than people do.

Keeping Kitty Content

Does it seem as if your cat wraps his front paws around your calf each time you try to leave the house? He may have a case of separation anxiety. Show him how much you care for his welfare by following these helpful hints.

Don't make a big deal about exiting or entering. Sadly, we're the reason why some cats make such a fuss about bidding us bye-bye or hugging us hello. We're flattered by the shower of attention. To stop clingy behavior when you enter, ignore your cat for a few minutes. Or reach for a toy mouse stashed in a basket by the door. Throw it as soon as you step inside. Your cat will learn to unleash his energy on the toy, not you.

Stage dress rehearsals. Spend five minutes sitting in a chair with your cat by your side. Don't talk to him or touch him. Do this to put him in a calm state. Then stand up, pick up your car keys, and walk outside out of sight for a minute or so. Re-enter the house and again ignore your cat. Wait a few minutes before greeting him by name in a casual tone. Gradually build up these practices to 10 or 15 minutes.

Occupy your cat's solo time by filling special treat balls (available at pet stores) and hiding them around the house. While you're away, your cat can hone her predatory drive. She will focus on the hunt and not have the time or desire to destroy things out of boredom or anxiety.

Keep the radio playing on low. Some cats like jazz; others prefer talk radio.

Set the timer to turn on the television for 15 minutes. Set the channel to your cat's favorite show — maybe the Discovery Channel or Animal Planet. Or play a video with birds flying across the screen or mice scampering. Rent or buy *Babe, That Darn Cat, Homeward Bound,* or one of the Austin Powers movies (which feature the fur-free Mr. Bigglesworth).

Invite trusted neighbors or friends to stop by and play with your cat.

Telephone your home twice a day and leave a friendly message for your cat on the answering machine. Sample: "Hey, Callie, how's my good cat doing? You're the number one cat in the world. Be home soon." Be sure the volume on your machine is turned up so your cat can hear it.

46

Meowy Christmas and other Holidays

Cats don't know the true meaning of Christmas or Hanukkah or Kwanza. They can't fathom why the neighborhood sounds like a battle zone during the 4th of July. Or why strange children wearing even stranger outfits are ringing the doorbell on Halloween while begging for — and receiving! — treats.

Tips for a Happy Holiday

Cat-proof your decorations. An agitated, frightened cat may topple lighted candles in pumpkins and start a fire. Dangling witches and scarecrows can be tempting to curious cats, who may ingest the material.

Keep your anxious cat in a quiet part of the house during holiday parties.

Treat your kitty with a Christmas or Hanukkah stocking filled with catnip, toy mice, and cat treats.

Skip the tinsel on the Christmas tree. Its shininess is too tempting for your cat, who may accidentally ingest and choke on it.

Pamper your cat during anxiety-filled holidays by giving her plenty of reassuring TLC.

Don't get caught up in the holiday spirit and force your cat to wear a bow around his neck; he can trip or strangle on it. A better option is to buy him a new collar in cheery holiday colors at a fashion-conscious pet store.

Keep all cherished holiday ornaments, statues, and treasures out of paw's reach.

Wait a week or so after the holidays to bring a new cat into your household. The holidays are stressful enough and packed with errands and activities. Wait until you've gotten back into your regular routine before heading to the shelter.

Keep chocolate out of paw's reach; it's toxic to cats and can cause vomiting, diarrhea, and even death.

Keep mystery gifts out of reach so that your cat doesn't chew them apart.

Buy only nontoxic tree-water preservatives and artificial snow.

Pine needles are poisonous — and so is the water at the base of the Christmas tree. Keep a lid on the water or be really safe and opt for an artificial tree.

Avoid edible decorations, such as popcorn and candy canes. A cat being naughty rather than nice can suffer a stomachache.

During Thanksgiving or other big feasts, don't share your meal with your cats. Bones can choke animals. The rich gravy and thick pies can cause stomachaches. Instead, treat them with gourmet cat foods to let them share safely in the holiday bounty.

Halloween can certainly be far from a treat for your cat. Kids dressed up in costumes shrieking "trick or treat!" ringing doorbells, and spooky background music are enough to frighten even the mellowest cat. Keep her in a separate room far from the front door.

10 Cat Commandments

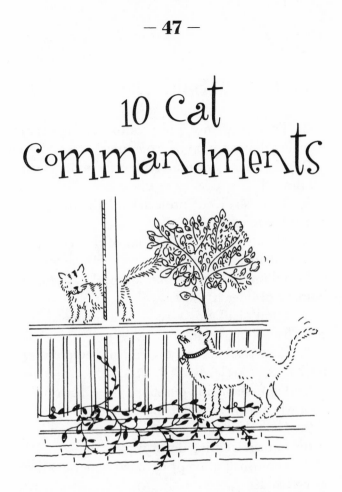

Who says cats don't have a sense of humor? A search on the Internet uncovered these 10 anonymously penned Cat Commandments. Whether they are obeyed is up to the cat.

And the Cat Said ...

1. Thou shall not jump onto the keyboard when thy human is on the computer.

2. Thou shall not unroll all of the toilet paper off the roll.

3. Thou shall not project hairballs from the top of the refrigerator.

4. Thou shall not sit in front of the television as if thou are invisible.

5. Thou shall not jump onto thy sleeping human's bladder at 3 A.M.

6. Thou shall not reset thy human's alarm clock by walking on it.

7. Thou shall not trip thy humans, even if they are walking too slowly.

8. Thou shall not push open the bathroom door when there are guests in thy house.

9. Thou shall not jump onto the toilet seat just as thy human is sitting down.

10. Thou shall attempt to show remorse when being scolded.

Super Supplements

Although manufacturers of commercial cat food are constantly improving and fortifying chow, cats don't always get the right amount of necessary vitamins and minerals. You can put the shine back in your cat's coat, fend off itchy skin, or assist muscle and joint function with supplements.

The Lowdown on Supplements

Before you start using supplements, discuss your cat's specific needs with a holistic veterinarian.

You can locate a holistic vet in your area by contacting the American Holistic Veterinary Medical Association at (410) 569-0795 or through its Web site at www.altvetmed.com.

ᘏ   ᘒ   ᘏ   ᘒ

Here are some popular supplements that can keep your cat in optimal health.

Acidophilus. This "good" bacteria detoxifies and fortifies the digestive tract and aids in the absorption of nutrients. Count on this supplement to treat diarrhea, gas, bad breath, and foul-smelling feces.

Amino acids. It may surprise you, but the biggest deficiencies in cat diets are amino acids. If you remember your high school science class, amino acids are the building blocks of protein that enhance hormone production, maintain healthy muscles and tissues, and keep the metabolism in harmony.

Antioxidants. To help you remember the top antioxidants available, think ACES: vitamins A, C, and E plus the mineral selenium. Antioxidants help fend off environmental toxins, lessen the risk for developing certain cancers, and bolster the immune system.

B-vitamin complex. Many cats come up short in the B vitamins, which are used to treat stress and cancer. In addition, B vitamins, specifically biotin and folic acid, provide energy for your cat. B vitamins convert carbohydrates into glucose, or blood sugar, and speed up metabolism. They also boost the immune system and help promote a healthy coat.

Biotin. This multibeneficial supplement aids in cellular growth, digestion, muscle formation, and skin repair.

Brewer's yeast. This natural source of quality protein, trace minerals, salts, and B-complex vitamins also helps repel fleas.

Calcium, magnesium, phosphorus, and zinc. These minerals work together to keep your cat's nervous system functioning at its best. They also fortify his teeth and bones. But be patient: Your cat must take these supplements for a month or so before you'll notice any beneficial results.

Cleansers and detoxifiers. Chlorophyll, algae, barley, wheatgrass, spinach, broccoli, and kelp bolster the immune system and cleanse the blood. These are ideal supplements for aging cats and for those recovering from cancer or surgery.

Cranberry. In capsule form, this supplement is good for chronic bladder infections.

Dl-methionin. An amino acid that helps keep the urine acidic, dl-methionin prevents crystallization and stones in the urinary tract.

Glucosamine sulfate and chondroitin sulfate. These supplements are effective in combating arthritis. They reduce joint swelling, improve circulation, and promote production of synovial fluid to lubricate the joints.

Omega-3 fatty acids. This type of fatty acid is helpful for cats with itchy skin caused by allergies.

Omega-6 fatty acids. This type of fatty acid helps restore shine to a dull coat and assists cell development in the brain and immune system.

Papaya enzyme. Clear the air of cat gas by feeding your flatulent friend this enzyme. It naturally breaks down gas-producing particles in the cat's digestive tract.

Vitamin E. This vitamin is helpful for arthritis, allergies, skin problems, and heart conditions.

How to Choose Supplements and Determine Dosages

Use these guidelines to figure out which and how much of a supplement to use:

❀ Take into account your cat's size, age, physical condition, and stress level before choosing a daily supplement.

❀ Always follow label directions and never give too much, which can potentially harm your cat and worsen a condition.

❀ Introduce one supplement at a time to your cat's meals. Wait one week to detect any differences in skin, hair, bowel function, or general behavior before adding another supplement.

❀ Make sure supplements are kept fresh by storing them in airtight containers.

49

'Net Surfin' With Your Cat

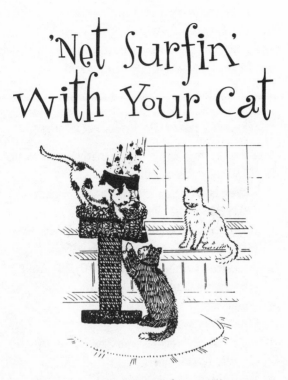

If you've got a computer and some time to spend on-line, try cruising some of the Internet's best and most popular pet sites. You'll find tips on care, medical information, and lots of product options.

The Best of the Web

Here are some of my favorite Web sites that cater to the needs and wants of felines:

🐈 Acme Pet, www.acmepet.com
🐈 Healthy Pet, www.healthypet.com

🐾 The Pet Channel, www.thepetchannel.com
🐾 Petco, www.petco.com
🐾 Petopia, www.petopia.com
🐾 Pet Planet, www.petplanet.com
🐾 Petsmart, www.petsmart.com
🐾 Petsource, www.petsource.com

IMPORTANT PHONE NUMBERS

Internet surfing can be informative, but sometimes you need personalized help.

🐾 American Association of Cat Enthusiasts, (201) 335-6717 (Pine Brook, NJ)

🐾 American Association of Feline Practitioners, (505) 888-2424 (Albuquerque, NM)

🐾 American Cat Association, (818) 781-5656 (Panorama City, CA)

🐾 American Humane Association, (303) 792-9900 (Englewood, CO)

🐾 American Society for the Prevention of Cruelty to Animals, (212) 876-7700 (NY, NY)

🐾 American Veterinary Medical Association, (847) 925-8070 (Schaumberg, IL)

🐾 Cat Fanciers' Association, (908) 528-9797 (Manasquan, NJ)

🐾 Humane Society of the United States, (202) 452-1100 (Washington, DC)

🐾 International Cat Association, (800) 842-2463 (Harlingen, TX). ICA lists purebred breeders.

🐾 PetFinders, (800) 666-5678 (Athol, NY). This national service helps find a lost pet.

50

Catty Remarks

True, cats can't speak words. But there have been many four-legged philosophers with an enlightening thought or two. And there have been some people, famous and anonymous, who have served supremely as cat interpreters.

Quips for Cats

There's no snooze button on a cat who wants breakfast.
— **Unknown**

As every cat owner knows, nobody owns a cat.
— **Ellen Perry Berkeley**

Dogs have owners; cats have staff.
— **Unknown**

Dogs come when they're called; cats take a message and get back to you later.

— Mary Bly

Thousands of years ago, cats were worshipped as gods. Cats have never forgotten this.

— Anonymous

Cats are smarter than dogs. You can't get eight cats to pull a sled through the snow.

— Jeff Valdez

There are two means of refuge from the miseries of life: music and cats.

— Albert Schweitzer

You might not like what they have to say, but cats will never deceive you.

— Lewis Carroll

If man could be crossed with a cat, it would improve man, but deteriorate the cat.

— Mark Twain

There are many intelligent species in the universe. They are all owned by cats.

— Anonymous

On the first day of creation, God created the cat. On the second day, God created man to serve the cat . . . On the seventh day, God tried to rest, but he had to scoop the litter box.

— Anonymous

Index

Acetaminophen, as poison, 9
Acupuncture, 74–75
Air travel with cats, 83–86
Allergies, 19, 75, 77, 93, 129, 130
Animal shelters, 105–106
Antifreeze, as poison, 17, 18
Anxiety, 49, 77
Arthritis, 31, 75, 77, 129, 130
Aspirin, as poison, 9

Bacteria, 14, 15, 32, 33
Baking soda, as cat shampoo, 47
Baths, 45–47
Beds for cats, 5
Behavior, 10, 18, 19, 43, 48–51, 55
Biting, by kittens, 43
Bitter Apple spray, 18, 51, 91
Breeders' associations, 132
Brushing, 111–113
Burns and cuts, 77

Cancer, 54, 55, 128, 129
Car rides. See Traveling
Carriers for cats, 36, 84
Cat Commandments, 125–126
Catnip, 103–104
Cat proofing, 7, 10, 17, 122, 123
Catwalk, installing, 5
Checkups, 9, 31, 36
Cheese
    as calcium source, 15
    as cause of diarrhea, 15

Chewing, 14, 18, 51
Chocolate, as poison, 16, 124
Choking, 50, 123, 124
    See also First Aid; Safety
Cold weather, 85, 102
Communicating with cats, 1–2, 3–4
CPR for cats, 58

Dandruff, 13
Declawing, 90, 91, 95
Decorating for cats, 5–7
Dehydration in older cats, 30
Diarrhea, 15, 77, 124, 128
Diseases, checking for, 9, 10, 36
    herbs for, 77–78
Doors, kitty, 24–25, 63

Emergencies, 7, 35
    national pet emergency hot line, 11
    See also Choking; CPR; First Aid; Injuries; Poisons
Exercise, 31, 37–39
Eyesight of cats, 4

Fabric, eating of, 10
First aid, 57–58
    See also Choking; Safety
Flatulence, 77, 128, 130
Fleas, 71–73, 77, 129
    disinfecting sinks after bath, 46

Food, 12–15, 107–110
  as flea deterrent, 73
  fussy eaters, 62, 63
  when traveling, 85
  See also Nutrition;
    Overweight cats

Games, 41, 52–53
  See also Play; Toys
Grass for cats, 5, 50, 77
Grooming, 111–113

Hairballs, reducing, 5
Health insurance for pets,
    114–115
Heat, 101–102
  keeping cats cool, 13, 81,
    82
Herbs for healing, 76–78
Holidays, celebrating,
    122–124
Home alone (cats), 119–121
Homemade meals for cats,
    107–110
Hotels, pet-friendly, 92–93
Houseplants, 5, 17, 50
Houses for cats, 5
Humane Society listings, 132

Identification, 22–23, 84
Infections, 77, 78, 129
  See also Bacteria
Injuries, 19, 27, 75
  massaging, 39
  See also Choking;
    Emergencies; First Aid;
    Safety

Kittens, 42–44, 51
  and catnip, 104
  and milk, 17
  as pets for cats, 67, 69

Legal considerations, 20–21
Litter boxes, 68, 81, 87–89, 92
Lost cats, 22–23, 65, 84, 117
  PetFinders service, 132

Massage for cats, 38–39
Medicine, giving, 9, 10
Meditation with cats, 29
Milk, avoidance of, 17
Motion sickness, 78, 79
Moving with cats, 64–66
Multicat households, 23, 67

Nails, care of, 26–27
Neutering and spaying, 54–56
Nutrition, 13–14, 15, 127–130
  for older cats, 31
  See also Food; Overweight
    cats

Older cats, 14, 30–31, 36, 129
  See also Arthritis
Outdoors, bringing in, 59–60,
    78
Overweight cats, 61–63
  See also Food; Nutrition

Pets for cats, 67–70
Pet sitters, 116–118
Pica (eating of fabric), 10
Pills, giving, 9
Plastic bowls, 14
Play, 41, 43, 44
  See also Games; Toys
Poisons, 10–11
  Acetaminophen and aspirin,
    9
  Antifreeze, 17, 18
  Chocolate, 16, 124
  E. coli, 14
  Houseplants, 17, 50
  National Animal Poison
    Control Center, 10–11

Pine needles, 124
Salmonella, 14
Salts, chemical, 102
Praying with cats, 97
Psychic, pet, 28–29
Pulse, checking cat's, 11

Recipes for homemade meals,
 108–110
Road trips. *See* Traveling

Safety, 16–19, 59–60
 during holidays, 122–124
 in hot or cold weather,
 101–102
 at sea, 95
 with toys, 99–100
 See also Choking; First Aid;
 Poisons
Scratching furniture, 49,
 90–91
 scratching posts, 49, 68, 91,
 104
Separation anxiety, 44,
 119–121
Shedding, 111–113
Sleeping, 6, 7, 40–41
 for older cats, 31
Smoking, 19
Sounds, cat, 1–2
Spaying and neutering, 54–56
Spirituality of cats, 28–29,
 96–97
Stretching, 37–39
Supplements. *See* Nutrition

Teeth, care of, 32–33
Temperature, taking cat's, 57
Toys, 6, 7, 98–100, 104, 123
 See also Games; Play

Training
 behavior, 48–51
 kittens, 42–44
 kitty door, 25
 leash, 60
Traveling, 79–82
 air travel, 83–86
 hotels, pet-friendly, 92–93
 leaving cats home alone,
 119–121
 road trips, 79–82
 at sea, 94–95
 See also Pet sitters
Trusts for cats, 20–21

Veterinarians, 8–11, 34–36
 associations, 132
 holistic, 127–128
Vitamins. *See* Nutrition
Volunteering at animal shelters,
 105–106

Water, 6, 13, 15
 bacteria in, 18, 32
 for older cats, 30
 when traveling, 81, 82, 85
 at sea, 95
Web sites, 131–132
 Doris Day Animal
 Foundation, 56
 holistic veterinarians, 128
 Humane Society of U.S., 17
 licensed veterinarians, 35
 pet health insurance, 115
 pet sitters, 118
Weight gain or loss, 9
 overweight cats, 61–63
 See also Exercise; Nutrition
Wills for cats, 20–21